MERTHYR
HISTORIAN

VOLUME FIVE

MERTHYR HISTORIAN

VOLUME FIVE

MERTHYR TYDFIL HISTORICAL SOCIETY
SOUTH WALES
1992

First Edition, September, 1992

© MERTHYR TYDFIL HISTORICAL SOCIETY

ISBN 0 9504845 5 5

Printed and bound in Wales by
WBC Ltd., Bridgend, Mid Glamorgan

INTRODUCTION

The Merthyr Tydfil Historical Society was formed in 1972 and celebrated its twentieth anniversary in 1992. To mark the occasion, the Society decided to publish Merthyr Historian, Volume Five.

The first four volumes were edited by Dr. Joseph Gross, who has retired as Editor but continues as a valued contributor.

Afon Taf School celebrated the 25th anniversary of its foundation in 1992 and Mr. Hugh Watkins, Hon. Secretary of the Society, has contributed an essay on the history of that fine School.

Dr. Trevor Herbert, Staff Tutor, Faculty of Arts, and Senior Lecturer in Music, at the Open University in Wales, delivered a fascinating lecture to the Society, on the Cyfarthfa Brass Band, and has supplied an essay on that Band.

Architect Mr. Martin Snead has provided an essay on Bryn Seion Chapel, Dowlais, based on a lecture he gave to the Merthyr Tydfil Historical Society.

Dr. Joseph Gross has written on The Development of an Urban Community in Merthyr Tydfil.

Mr. Josh Powell, well-known author, preacher and weather man, has provided an account of the terrible winter of 1947 in Merthyr Tydfil.

Dr. and Mrs. T. F. Holley have investigated the reception accorded Queensland Prime Minister Sir Samuel Griffith, when he visited his birth-place, Merthyr Tydfil, in 1887.

We conclude Volume Five with an essay by Mrs. Ann Lewis, on the Dowlais baritone vocalist, Morlais Morgan. It will be remembered that Mrs. Lewis, a serving Nurse at Prince Charles Hospital, provided an illustrated history of Merthyr General Hospital for publication in Merthyr Historian, Volume Four.

The Society wishes to record its thanks to these authors for their continued support and literary contributions.

Sincere thanks is also due to the staff of the Merthyr Tydfil Central Library, including Mr. G. James and Mrs. Caroline Jacobs.

T. F. HOLLEY
Chairman and Editor
52 Chester Close, Heolgerrig,
Merthyr Tydfil. CF48 1SW.

CONTENTS

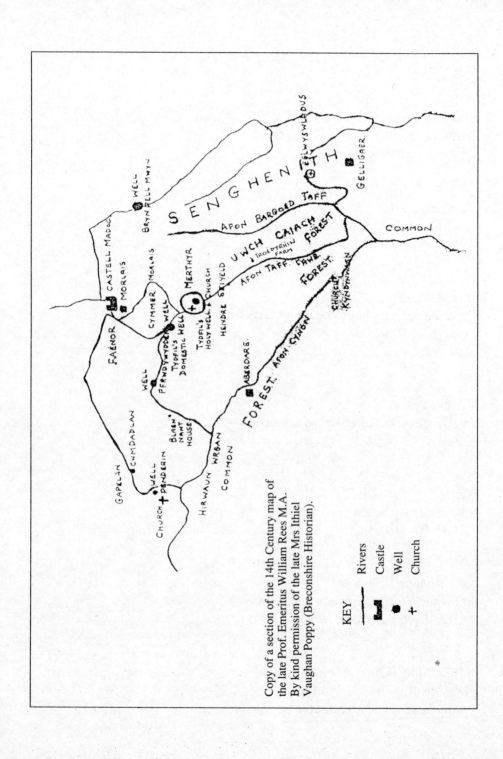

Copy of a section of the 14th Century map of
the late Prof. Emeritus William Rees M.A.
By kind permission of the late Mrs Ithiel
Vaughan Poppy (Breconshire Historian).

KEY

Rivers

Castle

Well

Church

A Valley Comprehensive— Afon Taf High School The First Twenty-Five Years 1967-1992

by HUGH WATKINS

Why Afon Taf?

In 1908, the famous Merthyr Historian, CHARLES WILKINS, published an edition of the History of Merthyr Tydfil with a reference to TROEDY-RHIW FARM, which along with the mill and PONTYRHUN BRIDGE, was one of the main features of the village of TROEDYRHIW, prior to its industrial development.

The ancient name of Troedyrhiw Farm (the site of Afon Taf High School), was 'TIR RHEOL GYMRWG' situated in the Hamlet of Taf and Cynon. The farm was part of the estate of IFOR AP MEURIG or 'IFOR BACH', born in 1100 or 1105 A.D., the Welsh Lord of SENGHENYDD, who in 1158 A.D. ruled over a wild tract of wooded, mountainous country from his stronghold, the site of the present CASTELL COCH, near Caerphilly.

The Lordship of Senghenydd was one of the cantrefi or sublordships of Morgannwg. It occupied a long but narrow stretch of land between the rivers TAFF and RHYMNEY and extended northwards from the sea at CARDIFF to the border of BRECKNOCK. The Lordship of Senghenydd was divided into three commotes:—

SENGHENYDD UWCH—CAIACH.
SENGHENYDD IS—CAIACH.
CIBWR.

Today, the districts of Merthyr Tydfil and Gelligaer, Caerphilly and Whitchurch.

The formal division of Senghenydd Uwch Caiach or Supra into the two constituent parishes of Merthyr and Gelligaer took place towards the end of the 12th Century, after the occupation of the Norman Lord of Glamorgan, Gilbert de Clare in 1272. When Ifor Bach became Lord of Senghenydd, he was entitled to collect the CYMORTHA or tribute of all the farms in his Lordship including 'TIR RHEOL GYMRWG'. The tribute was originally in cattle. After the Norman Conquest, tribute was paid to the Marcher Lords in coin. In Senghenydd it was payable on alternate years. In the 15th Century, on the second or third Tuesday after Easter. Troedyrhiw Farm was given to a Llewellyn Anwyl by Rees Vwya, a descendant of Ifor Bach, six centuries ago. Half a mile below Troedyrhiw, between the railway and the Taff, there is an old farm-house. A portion is in ruins and a general air of decay hangs around the whole. An old yew and other old trees surround it; the house is in a hollow, with the shadow of the mountains resting on it at early morn and in the evening. The thoughtful stranger looking at the old house and the small but high—walled garden in the rear, giving it a manorial character, would say this has been a place of importance in its time. Some substantial yeoman has lived here; some family of standing has been reared and sent forth into the distant world. What place is this? It is the old mansion of the IVORS. Five and six centuries ago it was in its prime. An Ifor lived there in state, Lord of a large tract of country, ruler over many serfs. In 1449, the owner of Troedyrhiw Farm was DAFYDD AP HOWELL, he paid a rental of 9d (3p) to the Marcher Lords. In 1540, Troedyrhiw Farm was occupied by a LLEWELLYN AP OWEN a descendant of MORGAN AP GWILYM AP MEIRIC of TIR-Y-GURNOS in Merthyr, when the Cymortha was 9d (3p) and 15d (7½p). Later it became the dwelling of the farmer of the PLYMOUTH ESTATE, succeeded by a Mr. T. Williams of Aberdare and finally for the last sixty years of its life owned by a Mr. William Nathaniel Jones, affectionately known to the people of Troedyrhiw as "Bill the Farm".

One of the ancient trackways of the Merthyr Valley was YR HEOL GYMRWG which passed through Treodyrhiw Farm. It crossed the Merthyr Gelligaer Mountain near Penddeucae Farm, dropped steeply in Troedyrhiw, crossing the River Taff at Pontyrhun Bridge which was probably well established by 1300 A.D..

In the Autumn of 1854, an English writer called GEORGE BORROW, who was on a walking tour of Wales found himself in Troedyrhiw. He wrote, "I left Merthyr about twelve o'clock for CAERFFILI. My course lay along the valley to the south-east. I passed a large village called Troedyrhiw or 'the foot of the slope', from its being at the foot of a lofty elevation, which stands on the left hand side of the road, As I proceeded on my way, the

2

scenery to the south on the farther side of the river became surprisingly beautiful. On that side noble mountains met the view, green fields and majestic wood."

Why was Afon Taf High School so named? This poem may give you the answer.

> For centuries it stood there,
> The farm at Troedyrhiw,
> In summer sun, and winter frost,
> When gales and breezes blew,
>
> Beside it CILFACH-YR-ENCIL,
> Reared its wooded head;
> Facing it the rounded CNWC
> Gleamed in the sunset red.
>
> Beside it sang old Afon TAF
> its ceaseless lullaby,
> And gave a peace and kindliness
> Which yet has not passed by.
>
> Among the urban uproar,
> By buildings old and new
> Still flows in peace and friendliness
> The Taff at Troedyrhiw.

What an apt site for a new school! To nurture young minds within such a historically rich past, and a geographically pleasing site, within the environs of their own homes.

In the early 1960's, a new word emerged into the field of Education, 'COMPREHENSIVE'. The all embracing, complete, extensive, fully inclusive school. Equal opportunities in Education would be on offer to all—with the final death throes of the dreaded 11+ Examination. No youngster would ever be classed as a failure. This as many other ingenious plans of its day was probably imported from our American cousins and their High School System.

In the early 1960's the then Ministry of Education requested each local Education Authority so submit plans to the SECRETARY of STATE for the

3

re-organisation of secondary education on Comprehensive lines in their respective area.

Mr. John Beale, M.A., the Director of Education, for the Merthyr Tydfil Education Authority at the time, stated, that the Authority was committed to build a nine form entry Comprehensive School at Troedyrhiw. This new school would have all the modern techniques available in the 60's and methods of learning. There would also be ample facilities for leisure, sport, with tennis courts, cricket pitch, rugby pitches and a running track.

The plan was to merge the three secondary modern schools in the lower Merthyr Valley and Quakers Yard Grammar School, producing a school population of between 1,300-1,400 pupils and staff of 75 teachers. The building was described as being "ultra-modern" and it was to be the first comprehensive school built by the Merthyr Tydfil Borough to replace the four existing schools.

Quakers Yard Grammar School had been founded in 1922, when members of the then education committee visited the ARMY, on SALISBURY PLAIN, a place which was then noted for its surplus of army buildings after WORLD WAR I, 1914-1918. The Committee decided to purchase army huts at a cost of £1,300 and acquire a plot of land at QUAKERS YARD for £700. The Junior Technical School was established in 1937 and amalgamated as a Grammar/Technical School in 1955.

PANTGLAS SECONDARY MODERN SCHOOL, situated in the village of ABERFAN had been built in 1906, to accommodate the pupils of Aberfan, Mount Pleasant and Merthyr Vale. In August 1940, the schools of Merthyr Tydfil were all re-organised. From 2nd September 1940, Pantglas Boys School became a Junior and Infants School and the Girls and Infants School became Pantglas Senior Mixed School until their destruction on that fateful day, Friday 21st October 1966—THE ABERFAN DISASTER.

TROEDYRHIW SECONDARY MODERN SCHOOL had been built in 1914, to accommodate the pupils of Troedyrhiw, Pentrebach and Abercanaid.

The oldest school was the TREHARRIS BOARD SCHOOL, catering for the children living in the extreme south of the Borough, at Treharris, Quakers Yard and Edwardsville. It was open on March 31st 1882, consisting of two departments, Juniors and Infants. In February 1896, the Junior Department was split into two, boys and girls taught separately. The two buildings then became known as:—

TREHARRIS GIRLS CENTRAL SCHOOL
TREHARRIS BOYS CENTRAL SCHOOL

The Initial Opening

AFON TAF HIGH SCHOOL was opened on August 31st 1967, with a nominal roll of 1,295 pupils drawn from the four schools.

QUAKERS YARD GRAMMAR SCHOOL—
Headmaster, Mr. D. W. Howells.
TREHARRIS COUNTY SECONDARY SCHOOL—
Acting/Head., Mr. M. Williams.
PANTGLAS COUNTY SECONDARY SCHOOL—
Acting/Head., Mr. K. J. Davies.
TROEDYRHIW COUNTY SECONDARY SCHOOL—
Headmaster, Mr. J. L. Lambert.

The Staff total was 72.

With some apprehension and excitement, we assembled in the largest building, the HALL of SPORT to be allocated with Form Tutors, pupils and respective classrooms, many of them still wet with paint, with new desks and chairs. Other classrooms had the entire stock from the four respective schools piled high on classroom floors. A wealth of text—books—hundreds of English, Mathematics, History, Georgraphy, Science books, soon to be distributed to the four corners of the School.

. We had to familiarise ourselves with the layout of the School, the endless corridors, twists and turns. The familiar cry "I'm lost, can you help me". The modern facilities not experienced in any of the four schools—well equipped laboratories, language laboratories, Sports Hall, gymnasia, Art block; a well—equipped workshop block with facilities for Woodwork, Metalwork, Technical Drawing, Building Techniques, Car Mechanics (all now termed C.D.T., CRAFT DESIGN TECHNOLOGY).

Can you picture a mass of pupils immaculately dressed from Years I to VI. Boys in black blazers, grey trousers, grey shirts for Years I and II; blue shirts for Years III and IV; and white shirts for Years V, VI and VII. Girls were similarly attired in skirts, blouses and cardigans. As it was said by one councillor at the time 'We now all wear the same school tie'.

Blazers were the fashion of the day and great pride was taken by all. Today the black pullover with school motif and outdoor coloured jacket like Addidas, Lorente, Torgan, Umbro and Diadort are worn. Black shoes were the order of the day, no trainers like Nike, Puma, Hi-Tec, Bebok, La-Gear and Troop.

Can you also picture 75 teachers all similarly attired in black gowns. The Headmaster of the day, the late Mr. D. W. Howells, had made it his first directive, that all staff at Afon Taf would now be one school, one staff, and no longer grammar, technical or secondary—modern but 'comprehensive' and we were obliged to wear academic uniform. Gowns meant status, we were like 'flitting batmen and women' moving from classroom to classroom.

Official Opening

1968, came the official opening, when the MERTHYR EXPRESS, of July 11th 1968, reported that Merthyr's £750,000 Afon Taf Comprehensive School was officially opened by Mr. Edward Short, MP, the then Secretary of State for Education and Science.

It was a very beautiful day, and the staff attired in their gowns lined up in two ranks from the school gates to the main entrance. This was achieved in true military form from the tallest to the shortest. Being of below average height—that of a true Celt—you can guess my place in the official line-up.

The day was a memorable one with the Minister officially opening the School at 2.30pm on Friday, 5th July, 1968. To quote the Minister "This new school has a close affinity with the Aberfan tragedy. This bright and gleaming school is in a sense a new beginning. It will make a fuller reality of education for children of all ranges of ability. Schools cannot do their job effectively for their pupils unless they change too, and if the change inside the school is slower than the change outside, then the schools will fall behind. The school curriculum must be receptive to and sensitive to what is happening in the world. Society itself would suffer if children left the schools unprepared for the World in which they will work and marry and bring up children of their own."

Catchment Area

The pupils who attend Afon Taf come from ten valley communities, villages steeped in coal mining traditions. Sadly, no more, with the closure of the pits in the area, namely, Merthyr Vale in January 1990 and Deep Navigation, Treharris, after 112 years of active mining life, on Good Friday, March 29th 1991, one of the oldest mines in South Wales. The pupil catchment area feeding Afon Taf covers an area of 18 square miles. Pupils travelled to school by buses provided by private contractors, public transport and by British Rail. From Abercanaid in the north with an adult population of 1,300; Pentrebach, pop. 1,200; the central area Troedyrhiw, pop. 2,800; Aberfan, pop. 3,000; Merthyr Vale/Mt. Pleasant, pop. 1,100; to the South,

Edwardsville, pop. 800; Quakers Yard, pop. 1,900; Treharris, pop 2,300; Trelewis, pop. 1,600 and Bedlinog, with a population of 1,500.

The Curriculum

The first year, 1967, the curriculum offered the pupils the following subjects: English, Mathematics, Physics, Chemistry, Biology, French, German, Welsh, Latin, History, Geography, Art, Music, R.I., Metalwork, Woodwork, Technical Drawing, Cookery, Needlework Craft, Homecraft, Engineering Science, Accounts, Office Practice, Shorthand, Typing. The traditional subjects as found in the old Grammar Schools, Technical and Secondary Modern establishments. The 1990's offer pupils a greater variety of choice. A Level—Advanced subjects: Art, Biology, Chemistry, Computer Science, Design, Craft Technology, Economics, English, English Literature, French, Geography, Geology, German, History, Home Economics, Mathematics, Music, Physics, Religious Studies, Welsh. Non-Advanced level subjects: Business Studies, Certificate of Pre-Vocational Education, Child Care, CDT Design and Communication (GCSE), CDT Design and Realisation (GCSE), Environmental Studies, French for Business, General Studies, German for Business, Information Technology, Media Studies. Office Skills: Shorthand, Typewriting, Word Processing, Physical Education and Sociology. Please note how the curriculum has changed due to the fact that Britain entered the E.E.C. Just imagine the mammoth task Mr. H. Davies, Deputy Headteacher, Academic, has of organising this extensive timetable. But all runs well, due to the efficiency of the administration staff.

The Friends

Although Afon Taf does not boast of a P.T.A. as such, since its commencement a small group of people have met once a month and worked extremely hard in trying to raise funds for the school. THE FRIENDS OF AFON TAF was formed on July 9th 1971, under its founder Chairman, Mr. E. Stanley Edwards. He became one of the school's great benefactors, until his sad death in 1986. Under its new Chair person Mrs. Joan Bennet, past Senior Mistress and its hardworking Secretary, Mr. Alan Evans, the Friends have organised the Annual Summer Fetes, Pottery & China Evenings, Glass Blowing, Fashion Shows, Musical Evenings, Lectures on relevant topics, like 'Drug Misuse'. Culminating in the organisation of a Bavarian Evening in October 1991, to launch the Silver Jubilee Year of Afon Taf.

STAFF 1967

HEAD MASTER:
Mr. D. W. Howells, B.Sc., A.R.I.C. (R) 1975 (D) 1990

SENIOR MISTRESS:
(R) Mrs. E. H. Powell, B.A.

HEAD OF LOWER SCHOOL:
(R) Mr. J. L. Lambert 1977

YEAR MISTRESSES:
(R) Mrs. M. K. Mills, B.A. 1984
(R) Miss C. Lloyd-Williams 1971
(R) Miss G. Evans 1984
(R) Mrs. D. V. Davies, A.T.D. 1983
(R) Mrs. A. Jones 1978

DEPUTY HEAD MASTER:
(R) Mr. J. H. Jones, B.Sc.

HEAD OF SIXTH FORM:
(L) Mr. F. L. Blackmore, B.A.

YEAR MASTERS:
(R) Mr. J. Hughes 1977
(R) Mr. K. Davies 1982
(R) Mr. C. Strange 1984
(R) Mr. M. Williams 1971
(R) Mr. G. Davies 1983

MATHS:
(R) Mr. D. G. Williams, B.Sc. 1982
(L) Mrs. J. M. Eatough
(R) Mr. S. Davies, B.Sc.
(●) Mr. Howard Davies, B.Sc.
(R) Mr. J. Powell 1981

MUSIC:
(R) Mr. S. H. Goodall, B.A., A.R.C.O. 1970
(R) Miss C. Hickey, L.R.A.M. 1990
(R) Mr. G. Davies 1983

METALWORK:
(R) Mr. D. G. Williams 1986
(L) Mr. D. Ramsay
(R) Mr. C. Stange 1984

WOODWORK:
(R) Mr. H. H. Davies 1976
(R) Mr. E. M. Howells 1985
(R) Mr. T. M. Jones 1978

CAREERS MASTER:
(R) Mr. G. Edwards, B.Sc. 1980

LIBRARIAN:
(R) Mrs. D. Evans 1980

AUDIO-VISUAL AIDS:
(R) Mr. E. M. Howells 1985

STOCK CONTROLLER:
(R) Mr. C. E. G. Davies 1983

MASTER i/c. PREFECTS:
(R) Mr. S. Davies, B.Sc.

ART:
(L) Mr. J. D. Lloyd, A.T.D. 1976
(R) Mrs. D. V. Davies, A.T.D. 1983
(D) Mrs. S. Jones, A.T.D. 1981
(R) Mr. R. E. Chandler, A.T.D. 1984

BIOLOGY & BOTANY:
(R) Mrs. J. Bennett, B.Sc. 1980
(L) Mrs. J. Williams, B.Sc. 1970
(●) Mr. J. Issac, B.Sc., Headmaster

CHEMISTRY:
(R) Mr. S. J. Evans, B.Sc. 1977
(L) Mr. R. Williams, B.Sc. 1981

COMMERCE:
(R) Mr. W. I. Jones, B.A. 1973
(●) Mr. G. Groves

8

DOMESTIC SCIENCE:
(R) Miss R. Adler 1990
(R) Mrs. J. Cuff 1970
(L) Mrs. J. Evans

ENGLISH:
(R) Mr. K. Edwards, B.A. 1975
(R) Mrs. E. Edwards, B.A. 1975
(R) Mrs. M. K. Mills, B.A. 1984
(R) Miss G. E. Evans 1984
(R) Mrs. D. Evans 1980
(L) Miss A. Knapp

FRENCH:
(L) Mr. L. C. Thomas, B.A. 1970
(R) Mrs. D. M. Francis, B.A. 1982
(R) Mr. E. A. Jenkins 1988

GEOGRAPHY:
(R) Mr. D. L. Campbell, B.A. 1984
(L) Mr. J. Acreman, B.A.
(L) Mr. E. Evans

GERMAN:
(L) Mrs. E. M. Davies, M.A. 1970

HISTORY:
(L) Mr. J. Garland, B.A. 1973
(L) Mr. I. Roberts, B.A.
(R) Mr. F. Vaughan, B.A. 1983
(●) Mr. H. Watkins

LATIN:
(R) Miss D. N. Williams, B.A. 1978

NEEDLEWORK:
(R) Mrs. E. M. Bassett 1977
(R) Mrs. A. Jones 1978
(R) Miss C. M. Jones 1977
(L) Miss M. Robbins

PHYSICS:
(R) Mr. R. Mills, B.Sc. 1984
(R) Mr. G. Edwards, B.Sc. 1980
(L) Mr. R. Stephens, B.A.

PHYSICAL EDUCATION:
(D) Mr. W. Eynon 1971
(L) Mrs. M. Scott Thomas 1971
(●) Mr. D. Flye
(L) Mr. R. Hopkins 1970

RELIGIOUS KNOWLEDGE:
(L) Mr. E. A. Stephens, B.A.
(L) Mrs. S. Hector, B.A.
(R) Miss C. Lloyd-Williams

REMEDIAL:
(R) Mr. C. C. L. Vaughan 1989
(R) Mrs. M. Hayes, B.A.
(R) Mrs. O. Sullivan 1981

TECHNICAL DRAWING:
(L) Mr. V. K. Preston
(R) Mr. K. Davies 1982

WELSH:
(L) Mrs. M. Rees, B.A.
(R) Mr. M. Williams 1971

SPORTS HOST:
(R) Mr. J. Powell 1981

SECRETARY:
(R) Mrs. E. M. Attwood

OFFICE STAFF:
(L) Miss S. Vining
(L) Mrs. L. Pierce
(L) Mrs. D. Vaughan

LABORATORY TECHNICAN:
(L) Mr. G. Edwards

WORKSHOP TECHNICIAN:
(L) Mr. B. Mullen

CARETAKERS:
(R) Mr. K. Bailey (Senior) 1973
(L) Mr. C. Preece
(L) Mr. R. Williams

CATERING STAFF:
(R) Mrs. E. M. Trehearne (Supervisor)
(L) Mrs. H. Green (Cook)
(L) Mrs. D. George (Cook)

GROUNDSMEN:
(L) Mr. V. Thomas (Senior)
(L) Mr. B. Lewis
(L) Mr. T. Lewis

KEYS: (R) Retired (L) Left
(D) Deceased (●) Still Servicing

9

Musical Shows

1972 saw the revival of Gilbert and Sullivan in the Borough with Afon Taf High School's production of the 'THE PIRATES OF PENZANCE' to capacity audiences in the School Hall on 2, 3, 4, 5 May 1972. The various school departments had co-operated in supplying costumes, lighting, sets, etc. The production was rehearsed and prepared in only one term and despite power cuts during the COAL STRIKE. The principal roles of "FREDERICK" and "MABEL" were taken by ROY DAVIES of Aberdare, a member of the D'OYLEY CARTE OPERA CO. and LINDA ADAMS (Treharris) a housewife, who had been soloist with the Dowlais Male Voice, Aber Valley and Treharris Male Voice Choirs. Other parts were played and sung by pupils and staff members. The following extracts are taken from the Merthyr Express of the time: "Spontaneous applause greeted the appearance on stage of the girl pupils playing the daughters of 'Major General Stanley'. Against the attractively lighted "rocky seashore" set, they were the personification of daintiness in colourful period costumes and "fruit pie" hats worn over ringlets and chignons. The "CONSTABULARY" evoked roars of laughter as they shambled on in antiquated uniforms led by their "SERGEANT", Mr. Eric Jenkins. "The Policeman's Lot is Not a Happy One" chorus was an uproarious success. The Constabulary consisted of Mr. Lyndon Casbeard, Terence Chewins, Mr. Russell Davies, William Evans, Philip Hamer, Ralph Handscombe, Kevin Jones, Terry Harfoot, Mr. Glyn Hopkins, John Hucker, Ian Richards, Mr. Cyril Vaughan, Mr. Hugh Watkins, Mr. Ronald Williams. As Frederick, the pirate apprentice, Roy Davies was in fine voice and acted with slick professionalism. He was well partnered by Linda Adams, whose acting and singing as "Mabel" was of a high standard especially her interpretation of "Poor Wandering One".

Mr. Glyn (later Head of Lower School) triumphed as "Major General Stanley" singing his way through the complexities of "The Very Model of a Modern Major General" with apparent ease. Mr. Jeffrey Lloyd (then Head of Art) was a suavely villainous "Pirate King", ably supported by his "Lieutenant" (Gareth James). Full marks were accorded to the band of "Pirates" in particular their performance during the "With Cat—like Tread" chorus when, while making enough din to wake the dead, the desperadoes boast of their stealth in carrying out their evil designs, a typically Gilbertian touch much appreciated by the audience."

All the qualities which distinguish the Gilbert and Sullivan operas including wit, spectacle and infectious melodies are in IOLANTHE, the fairytale cum political commentary performed on the 1-5th April 1974. "The younger pupils supplied the charm and freshness on the fairy scenes. The Seniors, Staff members, Friends, and past pupils the sophistication needed to point Gilbert's witty comments on Parliamentary procedure and the less brilliant aspects of the law. The story of a fairy married to a mortal acceptable even to the point of Peers of the Realm winged and cavorting outside the staid portals of the Upper House. Much teamwork had gone into the production, the delightful costumes made by staff and pupils showed up well against the scenic backgrounds produced by the Art Department, the impact being assisted by clever lighting effects. Past Afon Taf pupil Ann Beynon brough the touch of professionalism to her playing of "PHYLLIS", an Arcadian shepherdess and Ward in Chancery. She managed to reconcile artlessness with practicality. Phyllis was more than a match for the combined members of the House of Peers in this far from easy role. She displayed admirable clarity of diction when singing and speaking. She was well partnered by Martin Voyle as her half fairy, half mortal lover "STREPHON". Diane Launchbury made an excellent impression as a very attractive "IOLANTHE". Eric Jenkins scored an enormous success as the "LORD CHANCELLOR". He was admirably cast in a role which is a typical combination of Gilbertian wit and whimsicality. His solo, "See I to myself says I", was a triumph and later he soared effort-lessly through the tongue—twisting account of the horrors of a restless night. Memorable too was the singing of "Faint heart never won fair lady" by the Chancellor, 'the Earl of Mountararat' (Gary Bowden) and 'Earl Tolloller' (Haulfryn Rees). Barbara Fuller's fine contralto was heard to advantage in her role of the "Queen of the Fairies". Jeffrey Lloyd was extremely funny as "Private Willis", the Grenadier Guardsman on sentry duty outside Parliament. He gave a splendid rendering of the nonsense song about the "Little Liberals and Conservatives". Perry Thomas excelled giving an excellent performance as the "Chancellor's Page". Gillian Phillips, Sharon Hopkins and Janis Williams teamed well as the fairies, Leila, Celia and Fleta. Chorus work was splendid especially the Peers on the "Blow the Trumpet" item. A fine perfor-mance of Sir Joseph Porter, played by Mr. Eric Jenkins in HMS PINAFORE again brought further praise in 1976. A truly imposingly pompous figure whose tongue trippingly wound around the words of Gilbert's patter songs. Josephine, the gallant Captain Corcoran's daughter was the sweet voiced and attractive Mrs. Janet Green. Gwyn Mordecai was the Captain himself, Gareth Voyle his understudy. Ralph Rackstraw, the bold Jack Tar who loved a lass above his station was Haulfryn Rees. Little Buttercup was played by School

Secretary, Mrs. Mair Attwood and her under study Diane Launchbury. Ian Jones and the late Stephen Diplock and Tony Galliers were Ralph's shipmates in good voice for their high spots. Hebe played by Nicola Owen and Mrs. Marion Turner. Peter Beck and Mr. J. D. Lloyd alternated in the part of the villainous DICK DEADEYE. It seemed a shame to have to hiss Mr. Lloyd as he had designed the superb nautical set which transformed the whole of the front stage into a 'man o' war'. Just the right historical and nautical note was struck even before the audience reached the hall, for the decor of the school foyer included large copies of contemporary cartoons drawn by Mr. A. Osborne. The fine chorus of shipmates, sisters, cousins and aunts of Sir Joseph enhanced the performance, evidence of the hard work of stage director, Mrs. Kerri Mills, musical director, Mrs. Carol Hopkins, choreographer, Mrs. M. Williams and publicity manager, Miss Gwyneth Evans.

In April 1978, Afon Taf High School Operatic Society received a well deserved accolade, namely standing ovations for their five night presentation of Lionel Bart's musical "OLIVER". The ultimate in total involvement from office staff to THE FRIENDS OF AFON TAF, this kaleidoscope of mood from pathos to superbly controlled hilarity was professional to the degree of moulding inevitably innumerable details of production into a smooth arresting narrative punctuated by rich solo and choral work. Eric Jenkins portrayal of "FAGIN" must rank as a star performance. Dramatic and musical techniques were manipulated into a calculatedly controlled and realistic characterisation. To see was to believe in the Fagin. To many, outpassing the actor Ron Moody on the London stage. Verna Yoxall's mature "NANCY" was a delight only surpassed by her vibrant vocal work. Her compassion for Oliver and loyalty to the aggressive Bill Sykes was totally credible. Mark Williams well defined belligerent Sykes, whom his nightly audiences loved to hate and the sensitively controlled "BET" of Alsion Mordecai completed a dramatic trio of forceful impact. Mr. Bumble (Haulfryn Rees) and Widow Corney (a well padded Beverly Morris) consistently complemented each other in dramatic guile and humour. Alternating as "OLIVER", Kevin Lloyd and Geraint Smith extracted every nuance of pathos from the situation and unashamed tears from captivated audiences. The light relief of the "ailing Dr. Grimwig" played by Gavin Evans was extremely well controlled, while Stephen Diplock infused a realistic dignity into the role of "Mr. Brownlow". Donna Griffiths "Mrs. Bedwin" continued the warmth and dignity of the Brownlow household with a sensitivity which gave her comparatively short appearance an emotive impact. Perry Thomas "ARTFUL DODGER", was the ultimate in vitality and facial expression, emphasising the endearing artfulness of "Dodger" with the equally ultimate in professional restraint. This was a superb portrayal of a dramatic role fraught with pitfalls for the unwary. The trio of the dominating and the dominated was very finely defined by Ann Brown as Mrs. Sowerberry, Paul Williams as her long suffering husband and Catherine Jones as her truly caustic and undeniable "mother's daughter". The intimidating Noah Claypole and later intimidated innkeeper played by Ian Phillips was an excellent example of versatility and intelligently interpreted contrast. Urchins and adults provided an outstandingly unfussy, colourful melodic strength, each solo and choral presentation rising to a further peak of richness in tonal quality. A truly memorable production. All praise to producer Gwyn Mordecai who succeeded in integrating mood and characterisation into a totally credible experience for audiences irresistibly transported from tears to helpless laughter. Also in 1978 A. A. Milne's "The Wind in the Willows" was performed. In 1979 the school performed the "WIZARD OF OZ" and in 1981 "HIP, HIP HORATIO", "ROOSTER RAG" and "GLORIA" by Antonio Vivaldi. 1982 saw "HUMBUG", a musical play based on Charles Dicken's Christmas Carol. The school hall and foyer were decked out in Victorian manner to provide an atmosphere similar to a 19th Century County house.

The standard of performance, in all these productions, was always a credit to the ardent persistence of all involved in the attempt to achieve perfection, involving various departments within the school. Co-Producers, Mrs. Kerri Mills and Mr. Jeffrey Lloyd. Musical Director, Mrs. Carol Hopkins. Accompanists, Mr. S. H. Goodall (organ), Miss Ann Gough (piano), Mr. J. Gulliford (piano). Choreography, Mrs. M. Williams. Stage Manager, Mr. S. J. Evans. Stage Lighting throughout all these performances was in the capable hands of Mr. Ray Mills (Head of Physics) and his teams of senior pupils. Make-up, Supervision Mrs. J. Bennet, assisted by Sixth Form pupils. Scenery designed and painted by Mr. J. D. Lloyd assisted by Mr. R. Chandler, Mr. A. Osborne and members of the Art Department. Built by the R.O.S.L.A. Group under the direction of Mr. E. M. Howells and Mr. A. J. Turner. Properties, Mrs. D. G. Williams, Mrs. D. V. Davies, late Mrs. S. Jones, Miss H. Owen and pupils of the Art and Metalwork Departments. Refreshments, Miss R. Adler and pupils of Domestic Science Department. House Manager, Mr. J. Isaac. Administration, Mrs. M. Attwood, Mrs. K. H. Phelan. Publicity, Miss G. Evans. The shows became an intregal part of the village community and were always performed to appreciative capacity audiences.

In 1989, the Dramatic Society took on a new title, AFON TAF AMATEUR OPERATIC AND DRAMATIC SOCIETY. Under new musical directorship, namely, Head of Music, Mr. Jonathan Gulliford and Drama Organiser Mrs. Kathryn Thomas (English Department).

The aim of the Society is to involve as many pupils as possible in each production and to enlarge their musical and dramatic skills and appreciation. At Easter 1989, 'HALF A SIXPENCE' was performed, a British Musical based on a story by H. G. WELLS. 'Arthur Kipps', the poor apprentice played by STEVEN SLADE, his wife, 'ANN PORNICK' by LYNN THOMAS, supported by Michael Davies, Rhian Jones and a cast of 100. The production for Easter 1990 was the American Musical 'GUYS AND DOLLS', being performed with ANTHONY CHAMBERLAIN as 'NATHAN DETROIT' and LYNN THOMAS as 'MISS ADELAIDE' supported by Stuart Wiggins, Rhian Jones and a cast of 120. Christmas 1991, the American Musical was 'ANNIE GET YOUR GUN' with RHIAN JONES as 'Annie Oakley' and ANTHONY CHAMBERLAIN as 'FRANK BUTLER' ably supported by STUART WIGGINS and ELUNED PRITCHARD. Throughout each musical Mrs. D. S. Jones (Assistant Head of Middle School) and Mr. D. L. Davies (Welsh Department) two very accomplished performers have rendered admirable support. Also stage managers Mr. Byron Williams and Mr. D. Roberts. The Art Department under Mr. John Evans (Head of Dept.), Mrs. Susan Baber, Mr. Martin Baker and the CDT Department under Mr. Craig Johnson (Head of Dept.), assistants Mr. S. Beaverstock, Mr. H. Bevan, Mr. G. James and Mr. J. Mahoney, their skill and expertise have rendered the sets unforgettable. Front of House administration and advertising has been the care of Mr. Richard Thomas (Head of Upper School) who, with his team ensured that everyone had a comfortable seat. The Music Department in the charge of its Director, Mr. J. Gulliford have provided a fine chorus each year, supported by a first class professional orchestra.

School Choirs

The amalgamation of the four schools brought together a wealth of talent, one of the fields where this came to prominence was in the field of Music. Afon Taf Girls Choir first entertained in 1968 and has continued up to the present day being in constant demand both inside and outside the Borough. The first Head of Music was Mr. S. H. Goodall. In 1970 the Girls Choir was chosen as part of the musical programme at the WESTMINSTER HALL in

LONDON, part of the CENTENARY CELEBRATIONS of the EDUCATION ACT of 1870. Nine authorities had been selected. Afon Taf performed Gounod's "SANCTUS and BENEDICTUS".

The late Mr. S. H. Goodall retired in 1970 and was succeeded by Mrs. Carol Hopkins as Head of Music. The School yearly competed in the URDD NATIONAL EISTEDDFOD winning, in 1970, the SIR IVAN AP OWEN EDWARDS SHIELD, a most coveted trophy for the best Senior Girls Choir in Wales. In 1972 the School Choir was approached to form the background of the singing and acting in a sequence of a film production featuring SIR HARRY SECOMBE, called "A TOUCH OF THE SUN" the story of a Welsh school teacher in Australia. Most of the film was shot in Australia, Mr. Secombe came to the School to sing with the choir. The pupils involved enjoyed their experience.

Successive years and successive choirs have contributed to the success of Music at Afon Taf.

Under the Chairmanship of Mr. John Isaac, Headmaster, the School celebrated in magnificent style with a triple bill, in which the entire age range of pupils, staff and Friends of Afon Taf combined to provide a memorable contribution to Merthyr's ST. TYDFIL'S FESTIVAL, in 1980.

The Junior Boys Choir trained and accompanied on piano and organ by Mr. Jonathan M. Gulliford opened the programme's old Testament theme with Chris Hazell's "HOLY MOSES" with Brenig Gough as Moses and Jeffrey Roberts as Pharaoh. Clearly and in convincing costume, the choir unfolded the traumatic story with a confidence of vocal exposition and dramatic presentation which completely captivated its audience on both nights.

Under musical director, Miss Ann Gough, with piano accompaniment by Mrs. Carol Hopkins, the Junior Girls Choir provided a very lively "CAPTAIN NOAH AND HIS FLOATING ZOO" by Michael Flanders and Joseph Horovitz, with Jeffrey Roberts as Noah and Simon Beasley as The Lord. The combination of ancient themes, modern costumes and intriguing masks, coupled with the enthusiasm of dedicated choristers, resulted in a lively, visually compelling and musically captivating performance. The CREATION (part I & II) by Haydn under the baton of Mrs. Carol Hopkins with organ accom-paniment by Jonathan M. Gulliford soared to a superb climax of mixed choral exposition. Technical precision, musical tone, balance and interpretation combined to provide a stirring compliment to the impressive solo work of Artists Beti Jones (Soprano), David Leyshon Williams (tenor) and John Davies (bass).

Yet again Afon Taf sustained its reputation for the ultimate in special effects. Exquisite floral decor by John L. Evans and captivating mural representation for the triple bill by Alan Osborne, both of the school's Art Department, together with the major contribution by the lighting team led by Ray Mills of the Physics Department, masks for "Captain Noah" by John L. Evans and pupils of the Art Department.

The Ark built by E. M. Howells (later Head of Middle School) and pupils of the Woodwork Department, costumes by Misses A. Thomas and A. Williams (Needlework) and expert stage direction by Mrs. Kerri Mills and Mr. D. G. Mordecai (English Department) combined to provide a professionlism rarely experienced in school performances.

Each year there have been successful Carol Services first under the direction of Mrs. C. Hopkins and now under the present Head of Music Mr. Jonathan Gulliford. In 1983, "Holy Boy" was sung by the Junior Choir and Handel's "MESSIAH" by the Senior Choir.

Every Christmas, the Brass Band under its director Mr. H. Jones, has played and sung carols to the Christmas shoppers in the Merthyr Tydfil Precinct, also the School Orchestra, Wind Band and Brass Band.

Both Junior and Senior Orchestras over the years have given musical evenings led by Mr. Paul Storer, the string instruments teacher.

In 1986, Jeffrey Roberts, the Head Boy, was awarded the D. T. Davies Memorial Prize for Music, the award made by the Dowlais Male Voice Choir, he was later selected for the Welsh Youth Choir and is now gaining a reputation as a first class tenor. Mark Cheeke, Deputy Head Boy, was selected for the Welsh Schools National Brass Band. Anthony Cleaton was selected for the Welsh Schools National Orchestra. In 1988 became the first pupil from Afon Taf to gain a place at the ROYAL ACADEMY OF MUSIC, LONDON. Head Boy Steven Griffin won a Choral Scholarship to MAGDALEN COLLEGE, OXFORD. 1986 also saw 12 pupils being selected for the Mid Glamorgan Youth Choir, 5 pupils as members of the Mid Glamorgan Brass Band and 38 pupils became members of the Mid Glamorgan Orchestra at Senior, Transitional and Junior Level. In 1988 Music entered the field of modern technology when Electronic Keyboards and other electronic equipment was introduced to teach music. Afon Taf pupils today experience the up-to-date methods of making music. Also in 1988, 24 Afon Taf pupils, members of the Merthyr Schools Chamber Orchestra, entertained the citizens of Merthyr's twin town CLICHY-LA-GARENNE, to an Easter Concert of Music, in France. In 1989, the school choir took part in the massed choirs singing "MESSIAH" in RHYDYCAR on the 21st May with guest artists, Stuart Burrows, Selwyn Jones, Beverley Humphries, Annette Wyn Merriman as soloists and Roy Bohana as guest conductor. In 1989 Gareth Lloyd, Head Boy, became a member of the Welsh National Youth Orchestra. In 1990 the musicians of the school were invited to play at the opening of the Cellars of Cyfarthfa Museum. The official opening was performed by the well known T.V. personality ROLF HARRIS. In 1991 Eluned Pritchard became a member of the Welsh National Youth Orchestra. In 1991 the Senior Choir took part in the Joseph Parry 150th Anniversary Concert at Rhydycar on the 5th October. In 1992, Anne Cleaton, 6th Form pupil won the DORNAY CUP at the BATH ARTS FESTIVAL, for classical guitar playing and is a member of the South Wales Classical Guitar Society.

Under Mr. Jonathan Gulliford and his music staff, Mr. Emyr Roberts, Miss Naiomi Hitchings, Mr. H. Jones and Mr. P. Storer, and Miss Vanessa Bryant considerable successes have been gained in examinations offered by the Associated Board of The Royal Schools of Music. Practical examinations are offered in Pianoforte, Violin, Viola, Violoncello, Double Bass, Flute, Oboe, Clarinet, Bassoon, B Flat Cornet, Flugal Horn, E Flat Tenor Horn, Trombone, Bass Trombone.

These achievements surely uphold the pride in which the former Heads of the Music Department would have accepted and would have congratulated their successors for the continuation of high achievement in their subject.

School Trips

The 1970's, 80's and 90's have seen school visits extend beyond all my dreams as a boy. In my day, all looked forward to the annual chapel outing to BARRY ISLAND. "How I remember those wet days eating a picnic lunch under the shelters". On a regular basis pupils of the school, under the able leadership of Mr. Gwyn Groves, have visited the more extensive holiday areas of Europe namely 1979 Folgaria, Italy; 1980 Germany; 1982 Switzerland; 1983 Valkenburg, Holland; 1984 Worgl, Austria; 1986 Zirl, Austria; 1987 Northern France; 1991 St. Valery Sur Somme, France.

Some of the most popular trips with the pupils have been the SKI-ING instruction courses organised by Mrs. J. Jones, Head of Girls P.E., Mr. Huw Gilson and staff, to the ski-ing slopes of Europe where parties of pupils have had enjoyable experiences visiting in 1976 Austria; 1978 Seppada, Italy; 1979 Folgaria, Italy; 1984 Cerler, Spain; 1988 Bulgaria; 1989 French Alps; 1990 Zell-Am-See, Austria.

By the Grace of God, good ski-ing instruction, good staff supervision, all returned to date minus plaster, bandages or broken limbs.

Every year pupils throughout the school have enjoyed summer excursions after the summer examinations.

January 1977 saw 52 pupils in Year 4 and 5 with four members of staff undertaking an educational cruise to the Eastern Mediterranean, visiting Malta, Alexandria, Cairo, Mersin, Rhodes and Athens. Throughout the years there have been school visits to a variety of places of interest: The Roman remains at Caerleon Gwent, visits to Longleat House, Lundy Island, Bristol Zoo, Pensycynnor Bird Gardens, The Three Counties Show, Malvern, Royal Welsh Show, Builth Wells, Shrewsbury Show. Historical Castles, Berkeley Castle, Raglan Castle, Caerphilly Castle, Windsor Castle. S.S. Great Britain berthed at Bristol. Shakespearean Productions at Stratford-upon-Avon. Welsh Folk Museum, St. Fagans, Bath (Abbey and Roman Baths). Oakwood Activities Park in West Wales. Royal Air Force Museum, Hendon. Thorpe Park and Drayton Leisure Park in the Midlands.

Easter 1992, 70 pupils accompanied by Mr. Gary James and nine staff visited the newly established ultra—modern European theme—park, that of EURO-DISNEY outside PARIS.

Speech Day

Probably one of the most prestigeous events of the year is the Annual Speech Day and Prize Distribution Ceremony, where achievements in both the academic and non-academic fields are acknowledged and pupils are awarded for their efforts.

There have been many guest speakers over the years, introduced by the Chairman of the School Governors, in the early years the late Alderman Claude Stanfield, C.B.E. and now County Councillor Trevor Richards. The first was in 1970, when the guest speaker was Miss N. Jones, B.Sc., Principal, College of Domestic Arts, South Wales and Monmouthshire, Llandaff. For the first time in the history of education at Merthyr, three of the Borough's Directors of Education occupied the platform at Speech Day, July 1972. Mr. John Beale, M.A., then Director, later Director of Education for West Glamorgan. The late Mr. W. T. OWEN, who was Director of Education for Merthyr throughout World War II (1939-1945) and the guest speaker Mr. D. Andrews Davies, predecessor to Mr. John Beale, who left Merthyr in 1965 after serving the Authority for 17 years, to become the Secretary of the Welsh Joint Education Committee until his retirement in 1978.

Criticising the motto of the school "Golud gwlad ei goleuder"—'The wealth of a nation is its lustre' as being smug and Victorian, he suggested the more appropriate motto would be "GOLUD GWLAD EI HIEUENCTID"— 'The wealth of a nation is its young people'.

Referring to the school's immaculate condition after five years existence Mr. Davies complimented the school to quote: "It is a great tribute to you pupils that you look after your school and respect it. It is such a clean school that were I a stranger, I would think I was attending the opening function. I have known new schools that looked old after six months—and new universities too."

The Headmaster spoke of the changes since the days when there was more respect for authority and certain social standards existed. "In the 70's young people wanted to think for themselves but they were subject to the pressures of the mass media with the possibility of indoctrination. Many today seemed to be unaware that there is a price to pay for everything and that there is no substitute for hard work."

Other guest speakers throughout the years have been: 1973 Mr. John Beale, M.A., Director of Education, County Borough of Merthyr Tydfil; 1976 Mr. John Gwyn Morgan, M.A., Welsh Representative of the Commission of European Communities; 1977 Mr. Raymond Edwards, F.T.C.L., F.L.C.M., Hon.G.S.M., Principal of the Welsh College of Music and Drama; 1978 Professor Gwyn A. Williams, M.A.(Wales), Ph.D.; 1979 Mr. J. L. Brace, M.A., Secretary to the Welsh Joint Education Committee; 1980 Mr. D. W. Howells, B.Sc., A.R.I.C., Former Headmaster of Afon Taf; 1981/82 Professor Glanmor Williams, C.B.E., M.A., D.Litt(Wales), F.S.A., F.R.Hist.S.; 1982/83 Mr. John Beale, M.A., Director of Education, West Glamorgan County Council; 1983/84 Mr. Ted Rowlands, M.P., Member for Merthyr Tydfil & Rhymney; 1987 Mr. E. Roberts, M.Sc., Director of Education for Mid Glamorgan; 1988 Dr. Bleddyn Davies (Head Boy of the school 20 years before); 1990 George Thomas, M.P., The Right Honourable the Viscount Tonypandy, 'Mr. Speaker'; 1991 Mr. Jeff Young, O.B.E., Technical Director of the Welsh Rugby Union and Mr. Robert Norster, the Welsh Rugby team manager.

1977 saw the appointment of Mr. W. Mansel Richards, as Deputy Head (Pastoral), formerly Mr. Richards was Head of History at Cyfarthfa High.

Under his direction, a House System was set up in the Lower School and the Sixth Form, later extended to the whole school. It was felt that there was a need for a competitive spirit among the pupils, that pupils should receive rewards and incentives in the way of silver and gold star awards, merit certificates culminating in CERTIFICATES OF EXCELLENCE, not only for academic achievements, but for good attendance, behaviour, helping the community, sporting activities, collecting for charity, what is termed the "HIDDEN CURRICULUM" the making of a better citizen.

The four houses were named after: (a) MADOG—a Welsh Prince of the 12th Century, the son of King Gruffydd in North Wales, believed to have landed in America about 1170 A.D., before Christopher Columbus. (b) BRYCHAN, the father of TYDFIL, the princess who was slain by Irish Picts in 480 A.D., and who gave her name to Merthyr Tydfil. (c) LLEWELLYN— the last of the Welsh Princes, slain at CILMERI near Builth Wells in 1282— the last attempt of the Welsh to gain their independence. (d) OWAIN GLYNDWR—who led a rebellion in 1400 A.D. against the English and will always be remembered as the most important Welsh leader to resist English tyranny and domination until his mysterious disappearance in 1412 A.D.

One of the most prestigious projects undertaken by many staff and pupils, led with great enthusiasm and dedication by Mr. Mansel Richards was the HERITAGE PLINTHS. This earned for the School the PRINCE of WALES AWARD for 1988. On Friday 18th April 1986 the Project was examined by H.R.H. The Prince of Wales at the Community Design Service Headquarters, Cardiff. Prince Charles showed considerable interest in this Community Project and congratulated the school, represented by Head Boy Mark Evans, and all who had contributed towards its development.

A few weeks later the school learned that the Project had taken First Prize in the National Westminster's Bank Project Response aimed at assisting the local community. A total of 36 comprehensive schools throughout South Wales entered the competition. Each school was represented at the awards ceremony held at the Crest Hotel, Cardiff. The first prize of £300 was received on behalf of the school by Mark Evans, Mark Cheeke and Lisa Berry. The objective was to place plinths bearing local information at sites in the villages of Pentrebach, Abercanaid, Troedyrhiw, Aberfan, Merthyr Vale, Edwardsville, Quakers Yard, Treharris, Trelewis and Bedlinog. The school was indebted to the then Manager of British Steel Dowlais, Mr. John Owen for his help, interest and support in casting the iron name plate for each of the ten communities.

The project took five years to complete, every detail researched by staff and pupils. Each plinth contained an interpretative plaque giving details of local events past and present supported by illustrations and maps. The village name, a 'croeso' message and badges of the Merthyr Borough and Afon Taf High School are embossed on cast iron plaques. The plaques are strong, unpretentious and easy to maintain.

The pride felt by these valley communities in their past and their hopes for the future are embodied in this scheme. Incidental stories, events, tales and oddities great and small which make up a living history have to be included.

Working on this project has increased the knowledge and understanding of their local environment for many Afan Taf pupils. In 1991 Mr. John Isaac, Headmaster, on behalf of the School, presented to the Merthyr Tydfil Borough Council, 10 framed copies of these plaques, which form the Gateway to Merthyr Heritage plinths. The gift was accepted on behalf of the Borough Council by Councillor K. Evans, Mayor of Merthyr Tydfil. The plaques are now on permanent display in the town's Central Library.

On Friday 4th July 1969, H.R.H. Prince Charles, visited Merthyr Tydfil on his triumphal procession through South Wales, after his Investiture as Prince of Wales. Head boys—Ieuan Bleddyn Davies, Ronnie Griffiths, Head Girls— Marion Williams and Anne Evans formed part of the guard of honour when a capacity crowd of 5,000 crowded the approaches to *Cyfarthfa Castle* forecourt to welcome the Prince. Later, the Secretary of State for Wales, Mr. George Thomas, M.P., presented two blue and white mini-buses to the School on behalf of the Abervan Disaster Fund. Headmaster Mr. D. W. Howells thanked the Minister, to quote:-

"Money is being spent on children in a way by which they can develop their full capacity. Facilities will follow the trend of modern education and education does not begin or end in the classroom and is not to be found only between the covers of a text book."

1969 saw teachers opting out of dinner hour duties and the appointment of Ancillary helpers, also the opening of the first Summer Festival.

In 1970 Afon Taf competed in the well known BBC T.V. Contest *'The Top of the Form'*, the first round between *Grove Park Boys and Girls School, Wrexham*. After a stringent tuition by Mrs. D. Evans, the School Librarian and English teacher, the team comprised Colin Ross, Captain, Paula Jones, Beverly Hatch, William Clee. Reserves, Tony Rickwood and Bleddyn Hancock. It was with pride that we heard the Quiz Master Geoffrey Wheeler announce *Wrexham 56, Merthyr Tydfil 61*.

The victory at Afon Taf meant playing a second round against *Luton Sixth Form College, Bedfordshire*. Although the team lost, the experience for the pupils concerned was invaluable.

Over the years like any other educational establishment Afon Taf has experienced its setbacks.

In 1972, the effects of the National Coal Strike were felt at Afon Taf, when coal supplies failed to reach the school. From 2nd February to 2nd March 1972, the school functioned for only 5th, 6th and 7th year pupils, when extra convector heaters were sent to the school to keep the pupils as warm as possible. Staff attended each day for normal hours and were asked to engage themselves in school work. Years 1 to 4 were brought in for one day each week to meet their teachers for discussion and to receive and return homework.

In 1974, the Boundary Changes brought two more villages within the confines of Merthyr Tydfil, namely *Bedlinog* and *Trelewis*. Bedlinog Secondary Modern School was opened in 1949. Its headmaster was the famous Mr. Fred Evans. B.A. who later became M.P. for *Caerphilly* in 1969. Originally the building was a *Girls All Age School* built in 1910, and opened in 1912, but this all changed in 1949, when it became a co-educational secondary school.

The Old Boys School at Oakland Street, Bedlinog, opened in 1892, educated all boys from 7+ to 14+ up to 1949. Then it became a Junior School.

With these Boundary Changes the Merthyr Tydfil Education Authority sadly came to an end, being incorporated into the Mid-Glamorgan Education Authority. A petition of 2,000 parents in the Bedlinog and Trelewis areas strongly protested to the *Caerphilly* and *Gelligaer Division Education Executive*, that their sons and daughters be sent to *Lewis School, Pengam*.

Once these parents realised that Lewis School, Pengam was to be a split site school, i.e. the Lower School being in Ystrad Mynach as compared with Afon Taf a purpose built school, the villagers of both Bedlinog and Trelewis accepted the change. September 1974 saw 263 pupils from both villages, with three teachers, Miss Crid Thomas, Mr Haulfryn Rees and Mrs Linda Morgan joining us at Afon Taf. These pupils soon settled into their new environment.

1976, the long drought of the Summer months without rain, resulted in severe water restrictions being imposed. With careful planning and stringent use of water, the school remained open. The pupils were constantly reminded with stickers, posters, etc 'How to Save Water'.

Ironically, on December 27th 1979, after severe floods, the school was partly flooded, due to water entering as a backwash from the water channels. Twelve rooms on the ground floor in the north western part of the building were flooded to a depth of some 8 to 9 inches.

While he was teaching Mathematics at Afon Taf, Josh Powell made good use of his secondary interest as "Merthyr's Weatherman". The school was kept informed of his weekly recordings and all schools in the Borough were circulated every month with a written recording of the meteorological conditions that existed that month. These were compiled at the weather station at Cwmbargoed which he has manned for many, many years.

Afon Taf nestling in the valley has experienced over the past twenty five years all kinds of weather conditions. The changing seasons—the freshness of the bright, breezy days of Spring, with the grounds of the school covered in daffodils and spring blossom. The halcyon days of Summer. The glorious colours of the Autumn, when the trees along the Taff and on the mountain slopes are a myriad of colours.

Winter when the top of *Cilfach-yr-Encyl* is often covered by low cloud and the CNWC engulfed in mist. The dark days with rain, ice and snow.

The 70s and 80s experienced several winters of severe weather of ice and snow. In February 1969, winter showed all its venom when a twenty four hour blizzard produced arctic conditions throughout the Merthyr Valley.

Saturday 25th February 1978, witnessed an Arctic blizzard as the final minutes of the International between Wales and Scotland at Ninian Park, Cardiff were coming to an end. By late evening South Wales had become Siberia, disrupting all means of transportation, stranding hundreds of people. Seventy mile an hour winds resulted in Wales waking up to a nightmare world not experienced for 15 years, with drifts of snow up to 15 feet high. Sixteen inches of snow had fallen during the night.

Blizzard conditions repeated themselves again in January 1979 and a late snow blizzard in April 1981.

It was the week of January 9th–17th, 1982, that Merthyr experienced the worst blizzards and freeze-up for decades, since the great freeze-up of 1947, with roads impassable, food supplies unable to arrive at the shops, road and rail transport at the standstill. The then District Education Officer, Mr. Eddie Roberts, later Director of Education for Mid Glamorgan, closed all schools, in order to keep the roads clear of children, so that snow clearing could proceed. He did not want children attempting to walk to schools.

In the outlying villages of the Merthyr Valley, drifts of snow, more than 15 feet were commonplace. 1,000 tons of salt had to be brought by heavy Army lorries from the ICI salt mines in *Cheshire* to relieve the iced-up roads of South Wales.

Links with the Community. Helping with Communal-Based Charities.

Afon Taf pupils have since the school's commencement shown a genuine concern for others less fortunate than themselves. Without the humanity being shown by succeeding generations of pupils all the "chalk, talk and technology" in the world would never succeed in producing worthwhile citizens. The school has a long established tradition of raising money for charity, with sponsored silences, readathon, sponsored swims, non-uniform days. Throughout the years, donations have been given to local and national appeals. The major disasters that have occurred throughout the World, natural and man-made, Afon Taf pupils have risen to each occasion. Contributions have been forwarded to:- Institute for the Blind; National Children's Home; Bobarth Cymru; Feed a Child (TEAR); Poppy Appeal; Talking Newspaper; Annual Mayor's Appeals; Annual Blue Peter Appeals; Save the Children Fund; Colombian Appeal; Macmillan Nurses; L.A.T.C.H.; the 1989 Armenian Earthquake Disaster; Asthma Appeal; Sandbrook House Support Group; The Sidmouth Donkey Sanctuary; The famine Disasters in Ethiopia, Somalia, Sudan and other parts of Africa; Spastics Society; Child Line; Annual Greenfield Pupils Party.

The political upheaval in *Rumania* caused great hardship to the population but Afon Taf pupils rose to the occasion in their endeavour to help. Pupils throughout the school contributed food, toiletries and medical goods, resulting in 80 large boxes being presented to *World Care* party driving to Rumania, from Merthyr Tydfil.

The senior citizens have not been forgotten by Afon Taf pupils. Resulting from an article in the local paper, the Merthyr Express of the Summer of 1983, how the elderly people of the locality resident in *Pentrebach House* had no visitors. Mrs Jennet Cook (Asst. Head Lower School) in charge of Girls, formed *The Afon Taf Friends of the Community*. A group of pupils of Years 1, 2 and 3 have entertained the elderly at Pentrebach House, Haven Close, Ty Pontyrhun and T. G. Bryngolau. The first concert was held at Pentrebach House in September 1983. The pupils dressed in 1930s Charleston Style. They sang old songs and there were many soloists and dancers. Successive years led in 1984 to a Song and Dance Show, followed by a pantomime 'Cinderella' and another pantomime called 'Shakespeare Rattle and Roll'. Each one thoroughly enjoyed and deeply appreciated by the senior citizens concerned.

Christmas time each year, the elderly received from the Charity committee a Christmas gift, over 250 pensioners in the catchment area received a gift

Troedyrhiw Farm Prior 1967. Site of Afon Taff High School.

Afon Taf High School, Troedyrhiw, main entrance.

Afon Taf High School, Troedyrhiw, hall of sport.

Afon Taf High School, Troedyrhiw, senior library with librarian, Mrs. D. Evans.

The staff of Afon Taf High School form a guard of honour for Ald. S. G. Edwards, J.P., Mayor of Merthyr, the Rt. Hon. Edward Short, M.P., and Counc. Claude Stanfield, chairman of the school governors.

Aerial View of Afon Taf High School, Troedyrhiw.

Staff at Afon Taf High School, 1967.

These Fierce-looking characters took part in the Gilbert and Sullivan operetta "The Pirates of Penzance", which was staged by Afon Taf High School.

A colourful picture of the cast which took part in Afon Taf High School's production of "The Pirates of Penzance". Mr. Glyn Davies 'Major General Stanley'; Linda Adams as 'Mabel'; Roy Davies as 'Frederick'; Beverley Hatch as 'Ruth'; Mr. Jeffrey Lloyd as 'The Pirate King'.

The cast of 'Iolanthe', 1974.

Cast of H.M.S. Pinafore.

1989 'Half a Sixpence' Steven Slade as Arthur Kipps. Lyn Thomas as his wife, Ann Pornick.

Cast of 'Annie Get Your Gun' 1991.

Annie Get Your Gun.

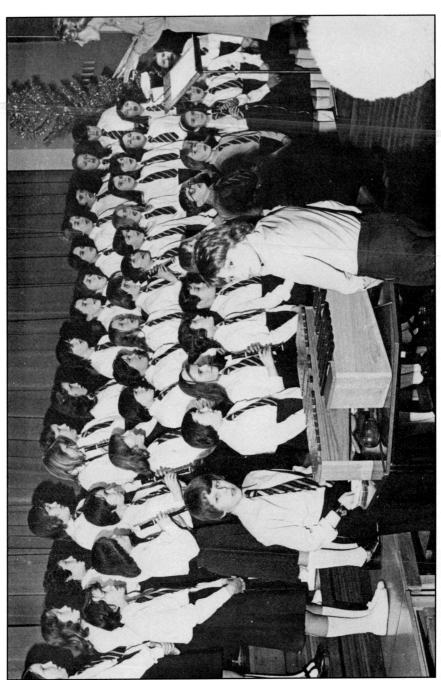

Junior School Choir, 1977.

School Orchestra.

Electronic keyboards. Music department, 1991.

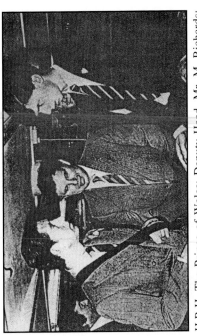

Directors Three, at Afon Taf High School Speech Day. Guest speaker and former Merthyr Borough Director of Education, Mr. D. Andrew Davies; Secretary of the Welsh Joint Education

H.R.H. The Prince of Wales; Deputy Head, Mr. M. Richards; Head Boy, Mark Evans.

Guest Speaker Mr. D. Andrew Davies (fourth from left) with the headmaster, Mr. D. W. Howells (third from left), the chairman of the governors, Alderman Claude Stanfield (centre) with officers, staff and friends at Afon Taf High School Speech Day, 1972.

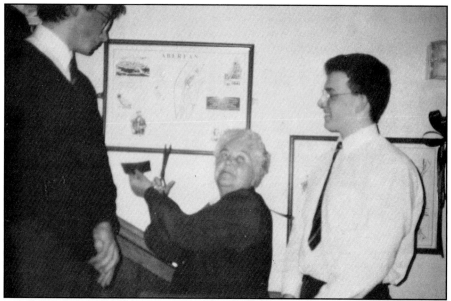

Councillor, K. Evans, Mayor of Merthyr, accepting framed copies of The Merthyr Heritage Plinths. Deputy Head Boy, Gareth Lloyd; Headboy, Andrew Elford.

Four of the Tops! Beverley Hatch, William Clee, Paula Jones and Colin Ross, of Afon Taf High School, who defeated a team from Grove Park School, Wrexham, in a 'Top of the Form' quiz contest yesterday. The record event will be broadcast next month. Afon Taf go forward into the quarter-finals.

Cancer patients will be helped thanks to the active social life of sixth-form pupils. A cheque for £278 was handed to the Merthyr Branch of Cancer Research Campaign on Thursday from youngsters at Afon Taf school. They raised the money by organising a party and other social get-togethers during their Christmas holidays. Pictured are CRC secretary, Pearl Carter, committee member, Pat Davey, with pupils, Anne Cleaton, Rhian Jones and school charity coordinator Roy Jones.

During the interval of an any questions evening recently held at Afon Taf High School, the chairman of the friends of Afon Taf, Mr. E. Stanley Edwards, presented the headmaster of Afon Taf, Mr. John Isaac, with a cheque for £1000 in aid of the school's mini-bus fund. Also in the photograph is Mrs. D. Brunt, treasurer of the friends of Afon Taf.

The Afon Taf High School History Group who won second prize in a recent 'Guardian' contest: from left to right, standing—Peter Jenkins, Brenig Powell, Mr. Fred Vaughan, Huw Rees, and Paul Evans; seated—Sharon Ford, Moira Powell, Jeanette Evans and Anne Harrison.

Afon Taf High School historical research group with masters, Mr. F. Vaughan, Mr. R. S. Evans and Mr. D. C. Roberts look over the new book they have produced, 1974.

The retiring Headmaster of Afon Taf High School, Mr. David Howells, bids farewell to Head Girl, Linda Jones, and Head Boy, Gary Bowden, at the end of his final term. Mr. Howells was previously Headmaster at the former Quakers Yard Grammar School. Also in the picture is his wife, Mrs. May Howells.

1991 Taff Vale Railway 150th Anniversary Mural. Compiled by Gywn Davies, Adrian Blackman, Neil Richards, Simon Jenkins and Graig James.

Afon Taff Select Rugby XV 1991–92.

selection box of biscuits and a Christmas Card, organised by the School's Charity Co-ordinator Mr Roy Jones.

Extra Curricula Activities/Achievements

In September, 1970, the then Head of History, Mr. Fred Vaughan. B.A. initiated what was to become a very flourishing Society, 'The Afon Taf History Research Group', a group of 26 enthusiasts, who researched into Merthyr's historical past. Its work included exploration of local sites, photographic recording, tape recordings, the collecting of a mass of information, plus old artefacts of interest from an old Victorian street lamp to railway sleepers.

In February 1976, the Society produced its first publication, 'An Historical Gazetteer of the Borough of Merthyr Tydfil'. In May, 1979, they produced their second published work, 'Recollections from Merthyr's Past', which was a best seller. In 1981, they entered the Annual Historical Competition for local history organised by the Merthyr Tydfil Historical Society taking 5 out of the 7 prizes.

Other Societies have flourished throughout the years enhancing the richness of the 'hidden curriculum'.

1976, the popular *Chess Club* was formed with Gwilym Hayes, winning the D.W. Howells cup for three years in succession.

The Debating Society successful debates have varied from *Call My Bluff* to *Mock Elections*. The Lower School Junior History Research Society, organised by Mrs. Jennet Cook. The Railway Society, under the guidance of Mr. D. Campbell, head of Geography and the Drama Society under Mr. Gwyn Mordecai.

In July 1975, Mr. D. W. Howells, B.Sc., A.R.I.C., retired as the first head of Afon Taf. He compared himself to '*Mr. Chips*', being one of the first pupils and the last headmaster of Quakers Yard Grammar School. Mr. D. W. Howells had played an important part in establishing comprehensive education in the then County Borough of Merthyr Tydfil and enjoyed his retirement until his sad death on the 13th September 1990.

Under its new head Mr. John Isaac, B.Sc., M.Ed., the school has gone from success to success and is now one of the foremost Comprehensive Schools in Mid Glamorgan.

In 1977, one of the most influential men in the field of education in the Merthyr Valley, Mr. J. L. Lambert, retired after a long and distinguished career. Headmaster of Troedyrhiw Secondary School, on amalgamation he became head of Lower School. He guided this section of school through Afon Taff's early years with expertise and succeeded in becoming Deputy Head, two years before retirement. He sadly passed away on 31st July 1986.

Since 1980, the Gideon Society's representatives have yearly visited the School to present to members of the *First Year* copies of the New Testament.

1987, pupils under the direction of Mrs. D. S. Jones, Health Education Co-ordinator, produced a banner for the nationwide, national *'No Smoking Day'*, and was awarded 1st Prize, a VHS Video Recorder which was presented to the School by Imperial Life Assurance, who had sponsored the event through *Tenovus* and *Heart Beat Wales*.

In 1987 Merthyr hosted the *Urdd National Eisteddfod*, the organisation in the hands of Mr. Mansel Richards, Deputy Head. Pupils from Afon Taf participated as stewards and hosts and were highly complimented for their demeanour and general behaviour. Mark Evans, Head Boy was awarded the Merthyr Rotary Club 'Pupil of the Year Award' and Mark Cheeke, Deputy Head boy was awarded the *Tydfil Prize* for his work for the community.

In 1990, the school won the poster design competition *'Keep Wales Tidy'*.

In 1990, a video film produced for *Media Studies* was shown at the National Film Theatre in London. This successful video film was based on a poem about one of the children in the Aberfan Disaster, and had already won three awards at the international award ceremony sponsored by the Institute of Amateur Cinematographers.

1991 saw two anniversaries being celebrated at Afon Taf. The 150th Anniversary of the Building of the Taff Vale Railway. Five pupils under my guidance produced a pictorial display measuring 10 feet by 4 feet, telling the story of the building of the Taff Vale Railway. This mural was on display for six months at the Cyfarthfa Castle Museum as part of the exhibition celebrating the Railway's 150th anniversary.

The second event was the 150th anniversary of Dr. Joseph Parry, when Mrs. Jennet Cook's play on the *'Boyhood of Dr. Joseph Parry'* was shown to an appreciative audience and was extremely successful. Anthony Chamberlain, 6th form pupil, fresh from his success in 'Annie Get Your Gun', took part in the National Youth Theatre Production *'The Birds'*, a Greek comedy by *Aristophanes*.

A touring company presented a very dramatic play called *'Too Much Punch for Judy'* emphasising the dangers of drinking and driving.

The responsibilities of the Head of a school in the 1980s and 1990s are among the widest ranging in modern management. Under local management, schools have become important financial enterprises; governing bodies have assumed greater responsibilities, public awareness has increased the scrutiny to which schools are subjected, and, more than ever before, they are accountable to their local community.

The *Education Act 1980* widened the membership of governing bodies and extended parental choice. 1982 saw Mr. J. Isaac having to contend with the first sanctions, NAS/UWT versus the Education Authority. Disputes arose again in 1985 and 1986. Sanctions imposed by the Unions resulted in pupils being excluded from school, teachers working strictly within their prescribed hours, pupils unfortunately had to be excluded.

The *Education* (No. 2) *Act* of 1986 altered the balance of power on governing bodies and vested responsibility in governors in fields such as the curriculum, pupil discipline and teacher appointment. Section 47 of this Act came into force on the 15th August 1987 with the Abolition of Corporal Punishment at Afon Taf, like all other schools in the British Isles.

In 1988, the Headmaster, Mr. J. Isaac, informed the staff about the contents of the National Curriculum at Staff Meetings. The Education Reform Act of 1988 brought about an important change in Education by bringing in a National Curriculum for pupils aged 5 to 16 in all state schools.

A national curriculum would guarantee that all pupils would receive an education which was broad, balanced, relevant to their needs and set in a clear, moral framework. Core Subjects:- Mathematics; English; Science. Foundation Subjects:- History; Geography; Technology; Art; Music; Physical Education; Modern Languages: Welsh. Tested at 7, 11, 14, 16.

The Education Reform Act of 1988, also required local education authorities (LEA's) to delegate management of school budgets to all maintained secondary schools and primary schools of 200 pupils or more. At one time L.M.S. meant to me, London, Midland and Scottish Railway, there is many a Headteacher, nowadays, whose only wish is that it meant the same and not the modern translation *'Local Management of Schools'*. Afon Taf's implementation of Local Management of its finances commenced on 1st April 1990.

In its White Paper 'Working Together—Education and Training', the Government stated that from September 1987, T.V.E.I. (Technical and Vocational Education Initiative) was to become a national scheme, giving all 14–18 year olds access to a broader and enriched curriculum. With a wide range of ability in modern sixth forms T.V.E.I. was opened to all pupils and attempted to cater for potential university students and also those pupils who are seeking additional qualifications in preparation for work.

Afon Taf in the 1990s can offer not only the traditional A level courses but courses of study leading to examinations of the W.J.E.C; R.S.A. Pitman's Institute; the National Association of Maternal and Child Welfare and the Certificate of Pre-Vocational Education (C.P.V.E.).

The *Music Hall* jokes and guffaws referring to school dinners have at last been laid to rest for on the 12th May 1980 a cafeteria service commenced in the school providing a very varied menu and the option given to pupils to buy what they wished, paying for what they select item by item. This is now in the hands of a private enterprise 'Term Three Catering'. It is only with parental consent that pupils are allowed into *Troedyrhiw Village.*

Business–Industrial Links

Modern technology calls for closer links with *Industry* in the 1990s. Afon Taf is no exception, having strong industrial school links with local factories and businesses. Blue Bird Toys, Dragon Parc, Abercanaid, Hoovers, Sekisui, etc.

1991, to mark 15 years of operation in Wales and to recognise its links with the local community, the Japanese Firm Sekisui U.K. based at Merthyr Tydfil Industrial Park, Troedrhiw awarded a £1,000 Scholarship to a pupil at Afon Taf for outstanding achievement and contribution to the life of the school and the community. Richard Williams, sixth form pupil from Treharris was the first recipient.

The Scholarship was presented to the School by the International President of the Company, Mr. K. Hirota at a ceremony attended by Mr. David Hunt, M.P., Secretary of State for Wales; Mr. Ted Rowlands, M.P. for Merthyr Tydfil and Rhymney, Mr. J. Isaac, headmaster, the Town Mayor and many other dignitaries.

A new subject *Economic Awareness and Enterprise Activities*, forms part of the curriculum for 16–19 year old pupils. Under the Head of the Economics and Business Studies Department Mr. Peter Jones, pupils now have experiences of the Business World, 22 pupils of the Sixth Form accompanied by Mr. P. Jones and Mrs. Helen Johnson visited in 1991 a seminar on *Business in Europe*, a weekend in *Paris, France.*

Also visits to the *Stock Exchange, Bank of England* and the *Houses of Parliament.*

In the summer of 1990, 37 senior pupils (Forms 4, 5, 6) and 4 staff attended a Young Reporters Course in France to learn about French Customs. In the summer of 1991, senior pupils and staff under the direction of Mrs. A.

Blake, Head of French Department, attended a French Study Course at Dieppe. In 1992, a similar exercise was undertaken by 30 pupils and 5 staff, this time spending Easter in Brittany.

Senior Art Students accompanied by Head of Art, Mr. John Evans visited both the Paris and London Art Galleries to acquire first hand experience.

The first twenty-five years have passed with major changes in the field of Education. The first pupils of our school would not have imagined being able to use *computers*. In those days computers, seemed like *science fiction*. Even the use of *calculators* was unheard of—some adults of the day thought that their use would only serve the purpose of making the brain lazy. Nowadays, a youngster's low mark in Mathematics may be due to a weak battery in his pocket calculator, or that the solar cells are malfunctioning.

Calculators and word processing were things of the future. These aids now form a major part of school life and now children are just as confident with the keyboard as they are with the alphabet.

Examination Successes

The new ideology of the 1990s is that the success of a school is judged by its examination results. The new word that is foremost is 'accountability'.

Afon Taf can pride itself on its results over the past twenty-five years. Its successes have far surpassed its failures. The school prides itself on its A level percentage pass rate, which is favourably positioned with that of the county and national average. To name a few of its successes, namely:-

1975, Susan Blackmore gaining English, History and Scripture with a distinction in Special paper, entry to University College, Cardiff.

1975, Gary James Bowden, Scripture, History, Geography with Distinction University College Aberystwyth. Elizabeth Francis, gained a place at Atlantic College and then at Somerville College, Oxford.

1979, Lynne Phillips, English, French, Welsh, University College Swansea. Gavin Hywel Evans, English, Geography, History, London Institute of Archaeology. Jonathan Isaac, Chemistry, Mathematics, Physics, Bristol University.

1980, Geraint W. Morgan, Biology, Chemistry, Physics, Welsh School of Medicine, Cardiff.

1981, saw sixth former, Beverley Morris gaining A grades in Chemistry, Physics and Mathematics and an open Scholarship, one of the highest awards, to read Chemistry at Somerville College, Oxford, and Jeremy Flye entrance to Jesus College, Oxford to read Law.

1982. Richard J. A. Beynon, gaining 3 As in Chemistry, Mathematics and Physics with two distinctions at the S level, entrance to Bristol University.

1982, David Huw Thomas won the Evan-Morgan Scholarship to Aberystwyth University—competition was from some 600 sixth formers from all over the Principality.

1985, Richard Groves, Head boy 1984–85 was awarded the Tydfil Festival 1500 Prize for 1984, gaining 3 Grade A passes and 2 Distinctions in Special papers, entry to Bristol University.

1988, Anthony Cleaton was successful in obtaining a place at the Royal Academy of Music, London.

Headboy Steven Griffin won a Choral Scholarship to Magdalen College, Oxford.

1990, Jason Carroll, Richard Williams and Paul C. Lewis each achieved three distinctions A. A. A2.

These are some of the outstanding successes, there is not enough space in this essay to mention by name the hundreds of boys and girls who have had success at C.S. E and G.C.S.E. examinations.

1984, Anthony Tanner was awarded the 1984 Individual Tydfil Prize for his work in the community, his bravery in rescuing an elderly pensioner from his burning home.

1982, Stephen Roberts, who rose to fame at the Welsh National Youth Theatre in their production of '*Under Milk Wood*' by Dylan Thomas, at the Sherman Theatre. He is now pursuing a successful film and T.V. career, as the taxi-driver in the Television Series '*We are Seven*'. Under his stage name Steven Spiers, his next portrayal is that of a gritty heavyweight boxer in a new stage play '*Facing-Up*'.

1981 Ian Jefferson was selected by the British Schools Exploration Society as a member of their geographical summer expedition to Iceland.

1981 Perry Thomas and Jaqueline Burgess were selected as members of the Welsh National Youth theatre.

1983, Timothy Jenkins was selected as one of the stars to take part in the HTV's production of the '*Rhondda Riots*'.

1983, David Huw Thomas was awarded the Tydfil Individual prize for his outstanding contribution to the good name of Merthyr Tydfil.

The Tydfil Prize is awarded annually for outstanding work for community and charity Work in the group 11–18 years category.

Afon Taf pupils have served both in the Falkland Islands War 1982 and in the Gulf War of 1991.

1992, Ex-pupil Janice Lang of the Special Needs (Remedial) Department has been selected as one of the twenty four young people chosen by the *Journey of a Lifetime Trust* for her bravery in coping with severely impaired hearing and undergoing major surgery, to follow the old *Silk Road* from *Peking* to *Pakistan*.

Sporting Activities

Afon Taf has always had a strong competitive spirit, with the amalgamation of the four schools, a wealth of talent was released in all the major sports. Pupils have represented the County in Netball, Hockey, Athletics, Soccer and Rugby.

Many a 'budding' soccer player, rugby player or athlete at Afon Taf can attribute their success to the encouragement given to them by Mr. Derek Flye of the P.E. Department, now Head of Middle School. In his time 'Derek' has been Chairman of Welsh Schools Soccer; Chairman of Welsh Schools Athletics; Secretary of the Under 18 Welsh Soccer and Secretary of Mid Glamorgan Athletics.

In 1968, Afon Taf had a successful Soccer team. Early successes at Afon Taf were Colin Crotty, Adrian Jones, Alan Evans, Gerald Ingram and Stuart Ford.

In 1969, Lord Aberdare presented the '*Guto Nyth Bran*' trophy cup to Susan James. This cup is presented each year by the President of the Welsh Secondary School AAA to the outstanding competitor. In the 1969 Games Susan James threw the Javelin 110 feet and in 1969 was regarded as one of the best prospects in the whole of Britain.

Susan represented Wales in the Javelin Event in the Commonwealth Games in New Zealand in 1974.

In 1970 Afon Taf's Under 18 Soccer XI Football Team won the *Ivor Tuck Trophy* for the whole of Wales, also winning the Under 13 Soccer David Beynon Memorial Shield, Under 15 Soccer Keir Hardie Shield and the Gron Griffiths Shield. Senior pupils Dilwyn Evans and Philip Ingram represented the Welsh Under 18 Eleven against Scotland.

In 1971 Terry Chewins and Kevin Jones won the first inter-schools dinghy sailing competition at the *Dolygaer Outdoor Pursuit Centre*.

July 1971 witnessed the sad death of Head of P.E., Mr. W. T. Eynon (Billy) on the Sports Field. Under the new Head of Dept., Mr. C. G. E. Davies (Jeff) (1971–83), Mr. Derek Flye and Mr. Wynford Jones —the 'dynamic trio'— more successes were achieved.

1972 the Girls Gymnastic Team under 15 took second prize at the Urdd National Eisteddfod at Bala.

1976 Coral Maybank represented the School in Hockey in the South Wales Senior School XI.

1978 Michael Vaughan played for the Senior School Boys County Cricket XI.

1980 the Guelph Technical College from Canada played against the 1st XV and 2nd XV Rugby teams. A school team from Rouen France played the 1st XV Rugby team. Andrew Nolan gained the first Under 15 Soccer International Cap playing against Eire.

1981 Jeremy Flye represented Welsh School Boys in Athletics. John Hancock became an International Swimmer. 1982, the Senior Girls Netball team became County Champions. There were eight County champions in the Athletics team. Christopher Barry represented the Welsh Secondary Schools in an International Athletics team. Philip Bufton (Yr 3) was the best in Wales in the hammer throwing event. John Hancock (Yr 4), Calvin Harris (Yr 6) was selected for the Welsh Swimming team.

1983 saw successes in rugby, hockey, gymnastics, netball and soccer.

1984 the Under 15 Soccer Team won the Celtic Press Cup. Pupil *Kevin Hamer* won an International Soccer cap (under 15) playing against Ireland, Scotland and England and now plays for Watford Football Club.

1985 Malcolm Poole was selected to play for the Welsh Schools Under 19 Rugby team tour of *Zimbabwe*.

Suzanne Evans, Michelle Naldrett and Tracey Ford were selected to play for the South Wales Hockey Squad.

Afon Taf has for many years had close links with *Cornelius Vermudun School, Canvey Island, Essex* and for many years there has been an annual exchange and rugby fixture with Afon Taf acting as host and vice-versa, giving our pupils an insight into the English way of life.

1987 saw 72 pupils from *Sir Bernard Lovell School, Avon*, experiencing life in a Welsh Valley community.

1986 Andrea Morgan was selected for the Welsh School Squash team.

Howard Ruberry received his Soccer Cap playing for the Boys Clubs of Wales. Gareth Abraham (6B) was the only school boy selected for the Welsh Youth Professional Soccer Squad and played in Belgium. Graham Gwyn became a final trialist for the Welsh School Senior Rugby team.

1988 Lloyd Wood played in the Mid-Glamorgan Under 17 Rugby team and Wayne Richards in the Welsh Schools Under 15 Rugby team.

1988 Howard Rubbery was selected to play for the Welsh Schools FA in Switzerland.

1989 Lloyd Wood and Wayne Richards were selected for the Welsh Schools Rugby Squad. Lloyd Wood captained the County under 19 Rugby team.

1990 was a good year for Athletics at Afon Taf. Hilary Davies represented Wales in the Javelin. Huw Thomas represented Wales as the County Hurdles Champion. Richard Scrivens was the Welsh Boys Discus Champion and Karen Misselbrook was a member of the Welsh Judo Squad. Afon Taf Senior Netball team became the County Champions. Andrew John and Huw Thomas represented the Welsh Schools at the International Athletics match at Meadowbank in Scotland. Lloyd Wood brought further honour to Afon Taf by playing in three representative games with the Welsh Schools Rugby team's tour of New Zealand.

In 1991 Adrian Tucker was selected for the Welsh Schools Soccer XI against the English Schools.

1992 Brent Hewitt was selected to represent Wales at the Under 18 level.

1992 saw Afon Taf's Select XV schools champions scoring eight straight victories through the season. P.E. Master and 1st team coach, Huw Gilson, commenting stated "The success has been a triumph for team work. The Pack consistently producing quality possession and the three quarters have been lethal in their use of the ball". A fitting triumph to end the season and commemorate the School's 25th Silver Jubilee.

These successes are just the 'tip of the iceberg' of the sporting achievements of Afon Taf over the past twenty-five years. Due credit must be given to the hundreds of boys and girls who weekly, year in year out, have taken part in sporting activities representing their respective houses in local and county competitions. This essay unfortunately is too short to mention them all.

On Wednesday 8th April 1992, to celebrate its 25th Anniversary, the doors of Afon Taf High School were opened to the general public. Parents, friends, councillors, school governors had the opportunity to see the work achieved by its present day pupils and witness some of the educational changes that are taking place during the last decade of the Twentieth Century. The guest for the occasion was the Welsh Comedian Owen Money and his wife.

A great deal has been achieved during the past twenty-five years. Past pupils have been proud of their school. Since 1967, 6,300 pupils and 150 staff have passed through its doors. Afon Taf has made its mark in the community.

What will the next two and a half decades hold? Who knows? It is up to the present pupils to take pride in their now well established school, to ensure the future by using the 'Comprehensive' system to the full, to make full use of its opportunities, so that Afon Taf can continue to supply the country with worthy citizens well educated in the field of their choice.

"Learn from the mistakes of others, you can't live long enough to make them all yourself".

Acknowledgments

1. Mrs. Susan Mead, School Secretary, Afon Taf High School.
2. Mrs. V. Carr, Reprographics Office, Afon Taf High School.
3. Mr. Norman Davies, Assistant Planning Manager, Town Planning Department M.T.B.C.
4. Mrs. Susan Barber, Art Department, Afon Taf High School.
5. Mrs Carolyn Jacob, Reference Librarian & Staff, Central Library, Merthyr Tydfil.
6. Mrs. Kathryn Thomas, Drama Co-ordinator. Afon Taf High School.
7. Mr. Rowland Thomas, Headmaster Bedlinog Primary School.
8. Dr. J. Gross, President, Merthyr Tydfil Historial Society.

Acknowledgments to Photographers

Mr. Robert Haines
The Merthyr Express
Music Department, Afon Taf
Miss Ann Gough
Meridian Airmaps Ltd., Sussex
Others unknown

'A Softening Influence':
R. T. Crawshay and the Cyfarthfa Band

by TREVOR HERBERT

In the summer of 1908 members of the Merthyr Borough Council turned their minds to a niggling problem. The Cyfarthfa Band, which had effectively been stripped of the patronage of the Crawshay family for more than thirty years and no longer enjoying the success and prestige that it once did, had petitioned the Council for help. More precisely the band looked to the Council to take them into Borough control. It was not a good time for the local authority to be taking on new responsibilities even if they were minor ones.

On July 24 the 'General Purposes' Committee was informed that 'Mr Crawshay was prepared to hand over to the town the Cyfarthfa Band which consisted of 28 instruments, 21 iron music stands and 291 books containing 842 pieces of music, upon condition that the name 'Cyfarthfa' was retained in the title of the band in perpetuity'. The offer was not received with unequivocal approval, there were matters that needed to be considered 'particularly with regard to questions of cost'. The General Purpose Committee, itself a sub-committee, decided on a course of action that has characterised Welsh local authority administration for most of this century. They formed a further sub-committee to which the matter could be referred. Less than a month later, at the meeting of the General Purposes Committee of August 11, after lengthy debate, it was resolved that the main recommendations of the report of their sub-committee be accepted and that the Band be named 'The Cyfarthfa and Merthyr Municipal Band', It was noted that the band had 26 players who were employed mainly at the Cyfarthfa and Dowlais works and Collieries and that the conductor was paid £30 a year.

The cost to the Corporation was estimated at £25 per year but provisions in the report ensured that all of the bands' material possessions became the property of the Council and the duties of the band were so defined that the Council got more than its moneys' worth. In the summer months they were required to play in public for a minimum of two evenings a week. The Corporation was to have first call on the band's services and the Band were not to accept engagements from outside promoters without the expressed consent of the Mayor and Corporation.

The band officials who were required to be present for interview on that evening were the conductor George Livesey, the secretary William Batty and Mr B Phillips, the treasurer. They must have felt some satisfaction as they left Merthyr Town Hall on that summer evening but at least one of them might have reflected on the occasion with a hint of sadness. George Livesey was nearing the end of his life. A life of considerable musical distinction. He had been a player and conductor for the period when the brass band movement was taking flight as one of the great popular musical forces of the Victorian era. In the small group of bands that shone out with some distinction the Cyfarthfa Band was one of the brightest stars. George Livesey and his father Ralph before him had witnessed the glory of the band for most of the previous half century. He could be excused if a morsel of bitterness inhabited his countenance as he sat before a group of councillors pleading for a measure that saved from total extinction the most famous, and possibly the first, manifestation of Merthyr's heritage of instrumental art music.

In 1860 the Cyfarthfa Band achieved its most conspicuous exposure when it won the first National Brass Band Contest at the Crystal Palace. That famous event is well documented and I will return to it later but by 1860 the band had been in existence for at least twenty years. The actual date of its formation is quoted and misquoted. I have revised my views on the matter at least three times. Margaret Stewart Taylor, in her book *The Crawshays of Cyfarthfa Castle,* states that the band was formed in 1844. This is certainly wrong as are numerous letters published over the years in the Merthyr press extolling the past glory of the band and quoting 1844 as the year of its foundation.

The earliest relevant primary source known to me that has unequivocal authenticity is a bill of sale contained in the Crawshay papers at the National Library of Wales, Aberystwyth. The bill is from the London instrument maker and dealer Charles Pace and is dated March 21 1840. It presents an account for £9.9.0 to Mr Robt. Crawshay for the supply of three keyed bugles with tuning slides. A related document in the same collection of papers shows that the bill was paid, but not very promptly.

Clearly then the band existed or was in the process of formation in 1840 but a different source dates the formation of the band as 1838 and though this source is slightly weaker I have regarded it, for a variety of reasons, as accurate. The source is 'A note on the Crawshays' published in the Merthyr Express on May 17 1879, the time of the death of Robert Thompson Crawshay. In it reference is made to the band.

> In 1838, the famous Cyfarthfa Brass Band was started, and we make no apology for introducing here some account of the origin and growth of this splendid corps of musicians, upon which Mr Crawshay looked with so much pleasure and pride before his first terrible affliction in loss of hearing, and indeed always after. Originally there were 70 members, and a man from Staffordshire came down to instruct them; but, being all novices in the art, they made much "sound and fury" without music. Mr Crawshay went to London and fell in with a Mr Berrington, one of the leaders of the orchestra of Her Majesty's Theatre, and three brothers. He engaged them to come down, and Mr Berrington weeded the 70 down to 24 and then set them in training . About the same time, Mr Francis Crawshay started a band at Treforest, where he had Mr Gratian, whom he picked up at Wombwells menagerie. Gratian left Treforest, came to Merthyr, and established the band, which, in his hands ,rapidly acquired proficiency, and skill. Shortly afterwards, Mr Crawshay being in London, at Vauxhall met the late Mr Livesey "old Raafe" as Ralph came to be called, father of Mr George Livesey, the present conductor . . . .

The attractiveness of this source is that it was created when the relevant facts were still comparatively fresh in the minds of those who had witnessed the setting up of the band. It also clears up some confusion about the type of band it was and in particular whether it really was a working class band or, as I have elsewhere argued a private band that was in some respects professional. The source suggests two stages in the bands' early history. The first stage was the formation of a large band of little musical merit which, apparently, didn't last very long. The second stage was the creation of a more carefully hued and selected smaller group of players who were musically literate and technically accomplished. The article goes on to explain that the developing virtuosity of the band was due not so much to the fruits of the labours of those from the original 'untutored' group of seventy players but rather to the importation of men from afar who were already established instrumentalists and were enticed to Merthyr by Crawshay.

> . . . There had been, and continued to be, jealousies in the band, as the native element did not at all relish the introduction of 'foreigners' but Mr Crawshay picked up class men wherever he found them, and in this way perfected his corps.

Crawshay certainly did 'pick up class men'. The members of the reconstituted 1840s band included players from London theatres, travelling circus troupes and individuals or even dynasties of distinguished amateur musicians from the north of England. Several of the names associated with the band are now well known in Merthyr-Livesey, England, Walker among them. Other musicians of distinction were the French arranger and infamous drunk George D'Artney and the ophicleidist Samuel Hughes. Hughes was born in Shropshire, recruited by Crawshay in 1858 with the enticement of a good job as a railway agent and was destined to become, by George Bernard Shaw's reckoning, the finest exponent of the instrument in London.

By the time Sam Hughes joined the band it was already acknowledged as the premier band in Wales. Though a correspondent to a brass band magazine later in the century (who turned out to be a member of the Llanelly Silver Band) reflected that Cyfarthfa could not be labelled a 'Welsh band' as it contained so many imported English players, it was certainly one of the most potent cultural products of new urban Wales by 1860.

The great brass band contest at the Crystal Palace Sydenham in July 1860 confirmed and exposed that status of the Cyfarthfa Band. It was a remarkable occasion. The contest was held over two days. It is not certain how many witnessed the spectacle but The Times estimated that over 22,000 were present on the second day. More than 40 bands competed on each day (*The Times* mentions 44 *The Daily Telegraph* 48). The competing bands were split into six groups for the preliminary contest, the best twelve on each day went forward to the final contest where they were adjudicated by eighteen judges most of whom were prominent professionals and army bandmasters. It was, according to *The Daily Telegraph* 'the first Contest of Brass Bands ever held in the south of England'. *The Times* which devoted as much space to the event in its issues of July 11 and 12 1860 as it has to the brass band movement since, noted that 'For a first experiment of this kind the success was quite extraordinary.

The first days contest was won by a new band from Yorkshire which had been formed only five years previous, it was called the Black Dyke Mills Band. The second prize was given to a band sponsored by the celebrated industrialist and philanthropist Sir Titus Salt—The Saltaire Band. *The Times* reported that the third prize was given to,

> the Cyfarthfa Band (supported by Mr Crawshay, and from the ranks of which the late Jullien obtained Mr Hughes the celebrated ophicleide, and other excellent performers-conductor Mr R.Livesey) [they] played a selection from Balfe's opera *The Bondman*.

On the second day no others matched the performance of the men from Merthyr

> The first prize-£30 in money, with a silver cup for the bandmaster, and a complete set of Boosey's Brass Band Journal, in 16 volumes, presented by the publishers, was awarded to the Cyfarthfa Band (conductor Mr R.Livesey), from Messrs. Crawshay's ironworks, South Wales. The piece selected for this band was Verdi's overture to *Nabucco*.

The day's events didn't finish until 9 o'clock, the band must have been exhausted by the time they reached home but their endeavours were well worth it. It wasn't just that they had won; they had won what might be regarded as the most important contest in the history of brass bands. It was, as I have said, the first event of its kind in the capital. The London audience and the assembled competitors drew in their collective breath with admiration at the deft musical skills that Crawshay's band exhibited.

Crawshay may not even have been present but the prestige he acquired by their achievement was not unnoticed.It was common in mid-Victorian Britain for middle class people to regard participation in musical activity as particularly virtuous. It was one of the pastimes accessible to the working class people that was classified as a 'rational recreation'. Those who sought to improve the moral and intellectual abilities of working class people were themselves the objects of respect and admiration. Up to that time Crawshay had demonstrated little ambition to better the lot of his workers. The evidence shows that the Cyfarthfa Band was to all effects and purposes a private band formed and sustained by him as part of the elaborate image that demonstrated his wealth and status. As I have already shown, the original, raw ,working men's band was quickly defunct and replaced with a more finely manicured and carefully selected corps of musicians. But the achievement of 1860 provided a good opportunity for Crawshay to exhibit an image of himself which would place him high on the list of the wealthy philanthropists and friend of the working man.

The most famous projector of this image was none other than Charles Dickens. Two months after the 1860 contest Dicken's magazine *Household Words* devoted several of its pages to an essay with the title 'Music in Humble Life' The article listed the values and progress of music among the working classes. With the sound of Crystal Palace still ringing in their ears the authors sounded their litany of the musical achievements of the lower orders in Merthyr Tydfil and attributed the remarkable achievements of its band to the kindly patronage of its most illustrious inhabitant.

> Another set of harmonious blacksmiths awaken the echoes of the remotest Welsh mountains. The correspondent of a leading London newspaper, while visiting Merthyr, was exceedingly puzzled by hearing boys in the Cyfarthfa works whistling airs rarely heard except in the fashionable ball-room, opera house, or drawing room. He afterwards discovered that the proprietor of the works Mr Robert Crawshay, had established among his men a brass band, which practices once a week throughout the year. They have the good fortune to be led by a man (one of the roll-turners) who must have had somewhere a superior education.

The article goes on to describe the music that the band were capable of playing and the pride that they drew from their achievement. But the greatest achievement was Crawshay's.

> . . . I have been told it cost Mr Crawshay great pains and expense to bring the band to its present excellent condition. If so, he now has his reward. Beside this, he has shown what the intellectual capacity of the workman is equal to, and above all he has provided a rational and refined amusement for classes whose leisure time would otherwise probably be less creditably spent than learning or listening to music . . . . The habits and manners

of these men appear to have been decidedly improved by these softening influences.

The private papers of RT Crawshay show that in the months following the Crystal Palace victory William Jones, his private secretary, had to deal with a number of requests for the bands' services. He guarded his ownership of it jealously. In September 1860 Mr David Jones of Britton Ferry was firmly chastised for advertising the appearance of the band in Neath when permission had not been obtained from Crawshay,

> I cannot imagine why such an announcement should have been made without first of all obtaining my permission. I have received your letter on the subject but I do not acknowledge the excuse sufficient for such a liberty . . . .

Those who took the proper course by requesting permission to engage the band were left in no doubt that Crawshays own use of them would always remain a priority. In March 1861 Mr Edward Lawrence took the precaution of asking for the bands services several months in advance. Crawshay's reply left Mr Lawrence in no doubt as to what the priorities of the band were

> The time arranged for your concert is rather a long time distant and I cannot tell whether my Band will be required for some purpose of my own or not so scarcely like promising it to you; but if you will run the risk I have no objection to allowing you the band . . . providing I do not require it myself for some other purpose.

The repertory of the band and sources relating to the private affairs of the Crawshay family show that the band was used to provide music for the elaborate balls that were frequent events at Cyfarthfa Castle. The band were also used as a musical backdrop for other festive occasions such as garden parties and flower shows. But, as time progressed there was a wider audience for the band in Merthyr. The broadening of the bands role in the community was caused partly by the sheer demand on them for their services to the extent that Crawshay simply couldn't control it, and also by the growing influence of the conductor George Livesey. The other cause of Crawshays relaxation of his strict control of the band (though he never relaxed it completely) was the onset of his deafness which was quite profound by the mid 1860s. His main distraction by this time had become photography, his personal account books show regular and substantial payments for photographic equipment.

It became much more common for the band to appear in public in the town's parks and by the end of the century *The Orchestral Times and Bandsman* attributed the introduction of Sunday band concerts in Wales to the Cyfarthfa band. The innovation was not of course without controversy but John Vaughan proposing a vote of thanks to the band for one of their appearances referred to their performance as a 'musical sermon'.

The bands' major period of greatness was between about 1850 and 1870. After that they continued to be a very fine band but they held no sway over the bands of the north of England. Their significance in the mid-Victorian period is that they were not just a fine band but that they offered an example of working class musical potential when the brass band movement was just gaining momentum.

In the early twentieth century, after the adoption of the band by the local authority they struggled along as musical functionaries for the borough council. The relationship was not, it seems, an easy one. The weight of the duties that were expected of them and the size of their fees were often subjects of contention.

This frequently led to headlines such as 'Cyfarthfa Band dissatisfied' in the Merthyr press. The intricacies of those arguments need more examination than I can give them here. It seems clear though that the duties expected of the band were such that it was necessary to pay the men for playing. They had become, in effect a professional band. It is difficult to avoid making a comparison between the way that the band was treated by the local authority and the way it was treated by Crawshay fifty years earlier. The similarity is striking. One cannot but feel for poor old George Livesey. A fine portrait of him hangs at Cyfarthfa Castle Museum. He looks resplendent in his uniform . His musicality is beyond question and, in truth, it is to him that the success of the band was due. It is a pity that he spent his closing years witnessing the decline of a band which, at its zenith, matched any in the world.

Trevor Herbert is Staff Tutor Faculty of Arts and Senior Lecturer in Music at the Open University in Wales.

"Mor hawddgar" . . .
The building, rebuilding and ultimate destruction of Bryn Seion, Dowlais

by MARTIN SNEAD

"Schism is often a sign of religious vitality" writes the author of the section on 'Protestantism' in the 'Encyclopedia Britanica'. Certainly the history of Nonconformity in Wales would confirm this assertion. For our purposes Merthyr Tydfil serves as an exemplar of this characteristic tendency of Nonconformists to split and reform, to quarrel and sulk and thereby produce a multiplicity of theologies and scores of places of worship wherein these philosophies and prejudices might be propounded. At the same time of course these chapels, however economical in their construction and however unambitious in their architecture, inevitably reflected and expressed the aspirations, ideas and limitations of their builders. The chapel was the public face of a religious group—the petrified presence of God on Street Corner or back lane. The ideals, the poverty and the pretensions of the congregation all find their expression in brick and stone, in plaster cornice and pitch pine pew.

The early development of Nonconformity in Dowlais is not easy to trace. The first Nonconformity congregation in the Merthyr Tydfil area was, of course, that which met at Blaencanaid Farm and subsequently at Cwmglo, eloquently described by Tom Lewis (Mab y Mynydd):-

"A dingle of sylvan beauty, it was screened by a profusion of dense copses and tall, overhanging trees where, tradition states, the nightingale often sang. But even in the delicious seclusion of Cwmglo the divesters were not free from molestation. Though their minds were fixed on the things of the spirit, their ears were always alert for the footsteps of the informer. A shaking bough, or a quivering bush, or the snap of a twig in the undergrowth, made their hearts beat faster, their blood run cold. The soothing influence of hymn and sacred song was denied them. Hostile ears might be listening in the thickets. On wintry nights, not for them the cheery gleams of a modern street lamp. The only light to guide their faltering footsteps was afforded by the moon or the stars. When the sky was overcast they stumbled over trackless mountains in an inky darkness that only country people know".

The chapel at Cwmglo was a simple building, similar in construction and general character to a modest barn. It was 30 feet long and 18 feet wide and was built on land owned by the Hensol Estate. A sixty year lease was granted in 1689. The small congregation at Cwmglo encompassed a wide range of theological opinions—generally however there were two groups—the Calvinists and the Armenians, the former holding more conservative views and the latter tending towards liberalism. For some time these two groups' views were reflected by the presence of two ministers who shared the pulpit, each supported by his own faction. The Armenians' Minister from C.1732 was Richard Rees of Gwernllwyn Isaf, Dowlais. He was born C. 1707 and had been educated at the Presbyterian College, Caerfyrddin (Carmarthen). Gwernllwyn Isaf was one of the three principal farms whose fields covered the area between the Dowlais and Morlais brooks.

(Gwernllwyn Isaf was near to the site of Gwernllwyn Chapel, now demolished, and Gwernllwyn Bach was on or near the site of the house of that name in Llewelyn Street). The houses at Gwernllwyn Isaf today are built around the much altered remains of the farm house where Richard Rees lived.

In 1747 Richard Rees and his Armenian followers left Cwmglo and founded the Hen Dy Cwrdd in Cefncoedycymer. He died in 1749 aged forty two, leaving a few hymns, some of which are still sung today. He, it can be fairly said, was the first Nonconformist of note from Dowlais.

Until the beginning of the Nineteenth Century the fields and pastures of Gwernllwyn Isaf remained very much as Richard Rees knew them. Although the first lease of land to build what became eventually the Dowlais Ironworks had been granted in 1748, growth was slow and somewhat spasmodic. In 1807 Josiah John Guest took over management of the works and under his direction considerable expansion took place. After 1830 the boom in railway construction resulted in orders for Dowlais rails from many parts of the World. To meet the demand the Ifor Works were constructed in 1839 and by 1845 the Dowlais Company employed 7,300 men, women and children, and could objectively be considered to be the greatest in the world.

In the wake of this expansion it was inevitable that the fields of the three farms would disappear—the demand for housing was insatiable and suitable building land on a hilly promentary between two streams was limited. However, some of the Nonconformists had a head start on the builders of shops and houses.

Around the year 1806 a chapel called Bethel was built by William Price, formerly Minister of Ebenezer Baptist Chapel (Plymouth Street, Merthyr). The exact location of this building is not known but it is reasonable to assume that Bethel Court at the lower end of Dowlais High Street was built on or near the site of this chapel. William Price's congregation of General Baptists, that is Baptists who believed in a more liberal, non-Calvinistic Christianity, eventually dwindled. At the same time there were a number of Independents living in Dowlias who were members of Soar and Bethesda chapels in Merthyr. In 1822 they rented the now vacant Bethel and thus formed the Congregation which would build Bethania. The first Bethania chapel was constructed in 1823, and opened in the Spring of 1824. This was a small building constructed at a cost of £400. The plot of land on which it was built was however substantial—extending between what would become known as Heol Bethania (later South Street) and Heol y Gwynt (Wind Street). In 1820 Caersalem Baptist Congregation was established, building their first chapel in the same year.

In the winter of 1825 to 1826 a dispute arose in Caersalem regarding the choice of a minister, some members maintaining that the man in question was too Calvinistic in his views. Perhaps they were former members of William Price's congregation, certainly their theology was similar to his. Approximately thirty members left and began to worship in a house in Church Street. Derisively they were known as 'Capel Back y Split' and for much of the Nineteenth Century Church Street was known as 'Heol y Capel' in commemoration of this little band.

Between 1822 and 1826 Bethania was served by Rev. Methusalem Jones of Bethesda, Merthyr (1822–23) and Rev. Samuel Evans of Soar, Merthyr (1823–26). They were followed by Rev. Thomas G. Jones who was ordained on March 23rd 1826. His first task was to oversee the building of a new chapel—the earlier chapel facing Heol y Gwynt was already too small for the growing congregation. This building facing South Street cost £600 and would be in its turn replaced by a much larger building eleven years later. Soon after the new chapel was opened, a dispute arose in the congregation regarding the Minister and in 1827, following a meeting of the Church which compelled him to leave, Mr. Jones and some of his supporters formed a new 'cause' and after worshipping for some time in a dwelling house, they used William

Price's 'Bethel'. It is apparent the Rev. Methusalem Jones supported Thomas G. Jones' case because he took charge of the congregation at Bethel for a period and was present in the meetings to re-open Bethel held on the 29th and 30th of September, 1829. But soon after this the Rev. T. G. Jones decided to leave the Independent denomination and become a Baptist. He left the locality and eventually became a tutor at the 'Athrofa Hwlfford' (Haverfordwest Academy). He achieved some fame, or perhaps notoriety, when he was the principal speaker at the Great Debate on Believers' Baptism held at Rhymni in 1841, where his opponent was John Jones, Llangollen.

Rev. T. G. Jones' replacement at Bethel was the Rev. John Morgan who was ordained there on 24th November 1830 and ministered until 1832.

In the meantime the congregation of 'Capel Bach y Split' in Church Street began to use Bethel as their place of worship, sharing the building with John Morgan's Independents but holding separate services. It appears that between 1826 and 1830 a representative of the Congregation of 'Capel Bach y Split', Henry Vaughan (after whom Vaughan Street was named), had been discussing with the owner of the land where Bryn Seion was eventually built, the possibility of it's purchase in order to build a chapel. Eventually on 4th August 1831, a lease of land was granted for construction of a chapel.

The first Bryn Seion, built in 1831–32 was a small building, holding, it is said, 300 persons. These figures are frequently exaggerated but it would be reasonable to suggest a lower maximum capacity—after all, the History of Bryn Seion describes it as being 'anghysurus o fach'. for many years it is recorded that only wax candles were used for illumination; the year in which oil lamps were introduced is not known.

It was in this small chapel so similar in character and amenities to Cwmglo, that the Baptists of 'Capel Bach y Split' found their new spiritual home. It was natural that they should now ask that they be recognised by the Baptist Association; however, their application was refused. It was at this time, and in response to said hostility that one of the Congregation penned the lines:-

"Er gwaetha'r holl elynion,
Yn wir Bryn Seion saif"

Although the two congregations had worshiped separately at Bethel, there had been some interchange between them, indeed their similar status as "outcasts" was bound to induce a sense of fellow-feeling. Following the Baptist Associations rejection it was natural that the beleaguered Baptists should turn to the Independents for support. It was decided that they would

46

unite and form one church. Some staunch Baptists were unable to accept this move and returned to Caersalem, but to the majority it was a logical development.

In 1833 to 1836 the Rev. Joshua Thomas of Adulam, Merthyr, had oversight of Bryn Seion. Then in 1836 Mr. Daniel Roberts, a native of Llansamlet, who kept a grocers' shop in Dowlais (although he had spent two years in the Neuaddlwyd Academy) and was a member of Soar, Merthyr, was invited to become minister of the congregation. He was ordained in Bryn Seion on 23rd of May 1836.

The normal approach to chapel building in the last Century, and indeed the early years of this Century, was to borrow, build and then pay back as circumstances allowed. This had been the means by which Bryn Seion had been build. By 1844 £200.00 remained of the debt incurred in building the first chapel twelve years earlier. The growth in population and the consequent growth of the congregation, meant however that the modest chapel was inadequate and it was decided to build a new chapel together with four houses. The total cost was £1,281.16s. 11d., including the £200 from the first chapel.

The opening services were held on November 26th and 27th 1844 and the building that awaited the animated congregation was certainly more spacious than its predecessor. there were seats for a congregation of 600. The architect was Rev. Benjamin Owen, Minister of Soar, Merthyr. Soar had been rebuild under Mr. Owen's direction two years previously and it is reasonable to suppose that the Minister-Architect's work was well thought of, as demonstrated by the invitation to design Bryn Seion. Daniel Roberts, Bryn Seion's Minister, supervised the construction work and kept the accounts. It should be remembered that until the 1880s the majority of building work was undertaken by direct labour, the client paying craftsmen directly. This method of working is, therefore, not necessarily an indication of poverty or an amateur organisation. Daniel Roberts' stipend was less than £1.10s. a month while the minister of Bethania received £5.00 a month. It is not surprising, therefore, that he continued to work as a grocer. Whilst the burden of debt remained on the Church there was little prospect of increasing the stipend. It was essential, therefore, to reduce the debt as quickly as possible. Inflation has so devalued currency that it is difficult to imagine the burden of a debt of £1,291. For 1990 values this sum would have to be multiplied perhaps by 10,000%. In the eleven years that followed the rebuilding a determined effort was made to clear the debt:-

		£	s.	d.
1842-43	Door to door collection	30	13	10
1844	Tea Party	67	16	2
1844	Voluntary offerings of the church	53	1	10
1844	Door to door collection	21	6	0
1845	Tea Party	106	11	0
1845	Door to door collection	18	13	0
1846	Tea party and door to door collection	103	9	0
1846	Collection in the "Cyrddau Blynyddol"	9	18	0
1847	Tea party, etc.	78	15	0
1848	Nothing collected	—	—	—
1849	Door to door collection and congregational collection	31	7	10
1849	Collected in Bristol by Mr. Roberts	43	6	4
1849	Lecture by Mr. Rees, Liverpool	26	19	6
1850	Door to door and congregational collection	20	0	0
1851	Lecture by Mr. Jones, Treforus	23	18	0
1851	Gift by Mrs. Margaret Price	3	0	0
1852	Door to door collection	20	0	0
1852	Gift by Mr. James Jones	20	0	0
1853	Tea Party	74	5	6
1854	Lecture by Mr. Jones, Treforus	28	19	6
1854	Door to door collection	18	0	0
1855	Voluntary offerings of the church	31	12	0
1855	Received from David Rees and Ebenezer Williams for use of gas from the chapel in their shop	6	0	0
		£923	19	3

The chapel designed by Rev. Benjamin Owen was a simple building, set back from the street (by then known as Bryn Seion Street). A paved way led to the chapel door, on each side were houses which were built up to the front facade of the chapel. It is reasonable to suppose that these were the houses referred to as being built in 1844 as part of the overall scheme for the chapel. Benjamin Owen's own chapel—Soar—was separated from Merthyr High Street by a number of small cottages over which it towered, and Capel Pont-morlais the famous Calvinistic Methodist Chapel in Merthyr had symmetrical cottages either side of its entrance physically attached to its main facade. Since these were two of the most influential chapels in their denominations, it was hardly demeaning for Bryn Seion to emulate them, and receive a little rental income as well. In terms of architectural design the effect was quite dramatic—a well proportioned two storey chapel rising behind and dominating a terrace of modest stone built cottages. At gallery level the window pattern was all important in the articulation of the facade—four windows equally spaced looked over the adjoining roof tops: and between the two central windows a plaque, above the front door reading:-

Bryn Sion

Ailadeiladwyd

1844

Later chapel design tended to concentrate on the detailing of the main, front, facade—variations of the Venetian window, highly decorative plaques, ornate rendering all contributed to a climatic front elevation, the sides and rear appearing nondescript in comparison. In the 1840's however the designers resources were limited, and in a town like Merthyr, the spirit of classical design, governed by symmetry, disciplined by exclusion and restrained by a sense of good taste, prevailed. Contemporary buildings—the superb Dowlais Market (1844), the finely crafted High Street Baptist Chapel (1841) and of course, Benjamin Owen's Soar (1842) were all confident expressions of an aestheticism which has its origins in the age of reason, and is far removed from the passion and romance of what came to be considered characteristic Victorian design.

Bryn Seion was rectangular in plan, but like Soar only just a rectangle—that is, it was a little longer than it was wide (Soar measures 66 x 63 feet). This was a logical plan—the function of the building was to provide a place for people to hear the bible, the prayers and, especially the sermon. There was no prayer book to follow of course and there were few hymn books. Many in the Nonconformist congregations were illiterate or semi-literate as suggested by the inability of the majority of Soar's trustees to sign the legal documents relating to the purchase of land for the construction of their new chapel in 1842. Hymns would be taught to the congregation by note until they could be sung from memory. Audibility therefore was of the first importance. Benjamin Owen had first hand experience of this—in Soar he created an amphitheatre second to none, where the dramatic interplay of pulpit and pew is given exciting architectural expression. The second necessity was illumination, although Bryn Seion had gas lighting from 1844, this was before the invention of the incandescent gas mantle and the light provided was not of a particularly high quality. Good, natural lighting was therefore essential. In the main facade, facing Bryn Seion Street were, as we already know, four windows at gallery level. In the side walls, to left and right were four windows at gallery level and four at ground floor level. The gallery extended around three sides of the chapel. At the far end, that is facing the main entrance, was the pulpit and behind the pulpit two long windows extending three quarters of the way down the rear elevation. This was a common arrangement in chapels of the time and echoed the earlier type of layout where two main entrances were placed on the long elevation, between which would be the pulpit, illuminated by twin three quarter length windows. (The only remaining example of this type in the locality is Carmel, Cefncoedycymer built in 1844). Clearly Benjamin Owen and his contemporaries were developing an established building form rather than pioneering a revolutionary change.

During the sixty years following the opening of the new chapel, this process of evolution continued. Advances in available technology, increases in expectations, changes in worship and the development of social activities connected with the congregation led to a series of renovations, extensions and improvements—made possible, of course, by a growing congregation whose disposable incomes gradually increased throughout the latter half of the Nineteenth Century. By 1855 the debt had been reduced to £368.16.4 /2. In 1857 the members were ready to meet the cost of a new ceiling, and painting the chapel, at a cost of £83. 19. 10. This ceiling was, I assume, that which remained in place until the final destruction of the chapel in 1969. There is no mention in the chapel History of its replacement. In 1862, the pews in the gallery were "rearranged", at the cost of £200. It is reasonable to suppose that for economy, in 1844 the gallery seating was of little more than a bench type, the seat backs being formed by the boarded balustrade which fronted the row above—with perhaps the front row having more "finished" panelled backs (as exists in the gallery of Ivor Chapel to this day). £200 was a substantial sum— Ivor Chapel was built fourteen years later for £400—so some structural work to the gallery may be included in the cost. The layout of seating may have been altered, together with perhaps some work to the staircases that led to the seating. The use of the word "rearranged"—(ad-drefu) in the official History in place of "renew" (adnewyddu) further reinforces this conjecture.

In 1876 a substantial schoolroom was constructed, attached to the left side of the chapel taking up part of the graveyard. Since the last burial had taken place in 1862, it is possible that exhumations were necessary in order to construct the schoolroom—it is unlikely that a large area of the graveyard would have been left unused with a view to building a schoolroom. If the construction of a schoolroom had been anticipated in the early 1860s, it is likely that the work would have been carried out sometime soon after 1862. We have already seen that the congregation of Bryn Seion, in common with Welsh Nonconformists of all denominations at that time, were not averse to borrowing should the need arise. The cost of the schoolroom—£320—was added to the small remaining debt and the church looked to the future.

In 1880 the ground floor of the chapel was rearranged and, to a considerable extent, replaced. There were two reasons for this: first, an out-break of dry rot, and second the feeling amongst the members that Benjamin Owen's layout of the ground floor was inconvenient and uncomfortable. To quote from the Chapel History (in translation):-

"Before the ground floor of the chapel was re-ordered, the seating around the door was totally different to the present arrangement:- (1) the two doors which now lead into the aisles from the lobby didn't exist at all (2) where the large lobby window is now there were two doors leading into the centre of the ground floor of the chapel, and at each side of these doors there were pews, and close to the centre of the floor there was a pew (*eisteddle*) facing towards these doors, there also was a "stove". This was a kind of heating apparatus, I should think, whose purpose was to reduce to some extent the effect of the cold wind and the bitter chill (*rhew deifiol*) in the winter which came through those doors, because the external and internal doors directly faced each other. We are not totally sure how the smoke escaped this stove. Some say that an iron or aluminium pipe led from the chapel to the outside wall, and that there was a flue in the wall leading to the "stack" on the gable. But now we know that that theory was incorrect, because when the stack was demolished in 1901, there was no way for smoke to go through it at all. The truth is that the "stack" was no more than an "ornament", built with bricks and capped with two large stones, each over seven inches thick. But although we don't know how, it is obvious that there was a way for the smoke to escape, because we find in one of Mr. (Rev.) Roberts' old books:-

"March 25th 1845, paid to John Edwards for wooden pipe on chimney 5s.6d; April 29th 1845 paid to Ann Morgan for zinc to make pipe for chimney 8s.9d; April 29th 1846 paid to Griffith Griffiths, tinman, for making the pipe 6s.6d."

By the stove, at each side, there were aisles running up to the two corners under the stairs where the gas meter is now and, on the other side, where the *llyfrau esboniadol megis Esboniad Mr. James Hughes a Geiriadur Charles ac eraill* "Expository books, such as Mr. James Hughes Exposition, Charles (Welsh) Dictionary and others" were kept for the use of the Sunday School—this is the evidence which was to be used to resolve every argument in the Sunday School; at each side of these aisles were pews".

This description isn't quite as illuminating as we might wish. It seems however that there was a central block of pews between the stove and the pulpit and that to each side the blocks were divided by diagonal aisles. Presumable these diagonal axes were not repeated at the side of the pulpit where a more conventional rectangular arrangement applied. Ironically the logic of this layout may have been based on the one central stove, having to heat the whole building and thus having to warm the incoming cold air as directly as possible.

The rearrangement involved the construction of a conventional lobby with symmetrical entrances to twin aisles leading straight to the sides of the "Set Fawr" and thus to the pulpit. The staircases to the gallery were also renewed, and it is reasonable to believe that this was necessary in order to provide enough space in the lobby for the new layout. It may well be that the windows on the side elevations lighting the half landings of the stairs were inserted at this time, but this is only speculation. Whether these windows dated back to 1844 or were a later addition, they were an uncommon feature—the adjoining houses, of course, prevented lighting of the stairs by ground floor windows in the front facade.

In order to ensure that dry rot did not re-occur, the level of the whole ground floor, including the pulpit, was raised by twelve inches in order to enable air to circulate beneath the timber floor. The "Set Fawr" was enlarged at the same time. We don't know whether any of the old pews were re-used or whether the entire ground floor seating was replaced, it seems however, that the old pulpit was retained and just reconstructed a foot higher.

We noted earlier that gas lighting had been in use from 1844. By 1880 the arrangements of thirty six years earlier were considered rather primitive and it was decided to replace the gas fittings at the same times as the ground floor was re-ordered. Before 1880 the lighting layout was as follows:-

"On the "Set Fawr" there had been originally two "uprights" and two on the pulpit, but these were subsequently moved, the two in the pulpit being placed on the wall behind the pulpit one each side of the marble memorial tablet and the two on the "Set Fawr" were removed altogether. Besides these there were three gas pipes at each side of the gallery and one under the clock (yr awrlais) to light under the gallery and the centre of the ground floor. On the gallery there were nine "upright" gaspipes, three on each side, two adjacent to the entrances and one above the clock".

The general effect on a dark winters night would have been gloomy, but the heat given off by the bare flames would certainly have supplemented considerably the heat of the central stove.

In the 1880 renovations a "Corone" was installed hanging from the centre of the ceiling. This contained 60 gas burners, and cost £25.00. At the same time the gas pipes were set into the walls—presumably to supply wall lights. All in all the improvement must have been considerable. Isaac Jones wrote in "Hanes Bryn Seion"

"erbyn hyn cydnebydd pawb fod yr ad-drefniad a wnaed
yn welliant mawr ym mhob ystyr"

Congregational singing was throughout the Nineteenth Century a matter for much debate in Welsh Nonconformist circles. The institution of the Gymanfa Ganu by Ieuan Gwyllt (John Roberts) in Bethlehem, Cae pant tywyll, in 1866, began a period of perhaps sixty years when music would play an increasingly dominant role in Welsh cultural expression, and ultimately create the myth of the "land of song". It became normal practice in chapels for the singing not only to be led by a precentor but also accompanied by a splendid organ. In new buildings the organ was often the most prominent feature, the pulpit which was theologically the heart of Nonconformity, playing a diminished role in the visual and spatial hierarchy. For chapels like Bryn Seion the addition of an organ was a fairly easy task—the improved artificial lighting made the two long windows behind the pulpit to some extent redundant. However, it was not until 1871 that a musical instrument of any kind was introduced—that was an "American Organ", purchased for £16 and chiefly used in the schoolroom. Soon after this it appears that the attractions of a pipe organ became irresistible and an organ chamber was built behind the pulpit—losing of course the two windows. The chamber cost £122, the designer (cynllunydd) being Mr. D. Davies, Garden House. The organ, which cost £280 and was constructed by Vowles of Bristol, was first played on 8th September 1894.

On the 6th July 1896 a young man from Llanrhystyd, Ceredigion, E. J. Rosser Evans, was ordained and inducted as Minister of Bryn Seion. Appropriately the ordination prayer was led by the Rev. John Thomas, Minister of Soar, Merthyr Tydfil, whose predecessor, Benjamin Owen had been instrumental in the construction of the chapel fifty two years earlier. The intervening period had been one of consolidation and growth, although in membership numbers Bryn Seion would always be overshadowed by Bethania and Bethania's sibling, Gwernllwyn. The three chapels were, in fact, within a few minutes walking distance of each other, but in a populous district where religion played a major part in many people's lives, it was not necessarily undesirable to have numerous places of worship. The tendency, particularly in the Independent denomination, was that individual congregations would develop a particular personality, varying in their social mix, and to a certain extent in the character of their worship. These differences are not perhaps significant to the late Twentieth Century historian made World-weary by a multiplicity of sects and pseudo sects each outbidding the other for exclusive possession of innate truth. But a hundred years ago things were more certain; because there was such agreement on the nature of basic Christianity, there was plenty of scope for minor differences and distinctions to occupy the front of the stage. In summary we might conclude that underlying the growth of Welsh Nonconformity were two essential certainties, one theological and one empirical: the certainty of theism and the omnipresence of death. The former made the latter endurable in a harsh but deeply integrated society. In this environment it is hardly surprising that by the turn of the century Welsh Nonconformists would look back on one hundred years of growth—both numerically and in terms of influence and prestige. This in turn generated a self confidence and ambition which would, in the first decade of the new Century, sustain a flurry of chapel building.

When E. J. R. Evans came to Bryn Seion the membership was 221 (remember that "gwrandawyr" hearers—or adherents—would have been present in some numbers as well), by 1902 the membership had risen to 274. The Minister's stipend was raised in 1899 from £8 to £9 a month in recognition of his and the church's success. At the same time further improvements to the chapel were initiated.

At the end of 1890 the incandescent gas mantle, a relatively recent invention which had considerably improved the quality of gas lighting, reached Bryn Seion. The "Corona" installed twenty years earlier with its sixty burners was replaced by six "clusters", each having four mantles, the Corona being sold for £3. In October 1901 the chapel debt had been reduced to £100 and it was declared that it was opportune to carry out further improvements. Thomas Jones of Walter Street was the Contractor. The work included the installation of a new ventilation system and the replacement of all the windows. The majority of the external render was renewed, a number of general repairs were carried out to the roof, the schoolroom was moved and a coalhouse and men's toilet were built. The total cost was £458 14s. 6d.

Between August 17th and October 19th 1902 the congregation worshiped in the Oddfellows Hall while further improvements to the chapel were carried out. David Davies was again the designer and supervisor of the work (for which he was paid 5% of the Contract Sum). The work was primarily connected with the main entrance to the chapel. As we know, there were two houses between the chapel's main facade and the street, the chapel doors facing a yard or "area" between these houses, the "area" being only a little wider than the door opening itself. Mr. William Williams, Bryntirion Street, was the main contractor in the work of building a roof over the paved area, and thus effectively moving the main entrance forward creating an outer lobby. The new doors were set under an elaborate pediment and were separated from the pavement by a telescopic gate. At the same time the interior of the chapel was redecorated, and the front of the gallery enhanced with mahogany and various, unspecified, mouldings.

Sixteen square yards of "tacelated tiles" were laid in the lobby paid for by eighteen individual subscribers who had been invited to contribute the cost of a square yard at fourteen shillings. The total cost of the improvements carried out in 1901 and 1902 was £953. 3s. 7½d. In 1903 the freehold of the land on which the chapel stood, together with the houses, schoolroom and graveyard, was purchased for £376. In 1905 dry rot was again discovered and treated at the cost of £15. 18s. 3d., and in the following year the graveyard walls were rebuilt at a cost of £13. 2s. 2d. Up to 1906 the total spent on building, maintaining and improving the chapel from 1844 onwards was £5,039. 7s. 7½d. This was a substantial sum, almost without exception borrowed, and paid back with some difficulty over a number of years. Chapel histories written in the early years of the Twentieth Century often make a particular point of the strenuous efforts needed to clear debts which were the consequence of sometimes over ambitious building programmes. In the case of Bryn Seion, however, the debt, apart from that in the years immediately following the rebuilding in 1844, was never excessive. The official chapel history does not lament the debt but rather displays a sense of pride in the achievements of a relatively small congregation, pride in the work that was carried out and the improvements made. Debt is faced squarely as a fact to be faced, a problem to be solved, a means to an end.

In 1906 the Rev. E. J. Rosser Evans left Bryn Seion and in the following year the Rev. D. Emrys James was inducted as his successor. 1907 marked the seventy fifth anniversary of the congregations establishment, and as part of the celebrations the Chapel's history was published. It would be perhaps inconceivable and certainly unbearable to the congregation of 1907, as they reflected on the past years of hard work and success, that the next sixty years would be years of contraction, disillusion and ultimately the demise of the congregation and destruction of its place of worship.

In a number of ways, with the benefit of hindsight, the writing was on the wall in 1907. The Welsh Language was in retreat in the South Wales Valleys, in retreat because it had ceased to be the medium of expression of a monolingual society. No longer was it *essential* to speak Welsh in order to buy goods, to work or to chat with neighbours. By 1907 Welsh was the language of the hearth, of the family end of the chapel, but English was the language of the local authority and the Government, the "novelette" and the picturehouse titles, the schools and higher education. In these circumstances it was inevitable that Welsh would become increasingly associated with the past— with old fashioned ideas, and old people. By the 1920s many Sunday Schools in Welsh Chapels in the Merthyr area were using English as their medium of instruction, the few children who spoke Welsh at home being grouped together in one class, sometimes regardless of age, and known by all as the "Welsh Class". Chapel services continued to be held in Welsh, and the older members, who spoke Welsh as their first language, used Welsh easily as their medium of social communication. Too often these same people spoke English to their children, or if they did speak Welsh to them, their children's grasp of the language often remained comparatively weak. The Welsh nation has long suffered a crisis of inferiority, a sense that all good and all authority lay outside its boundaries geographically "Man gwyn Man Draw"—or culturally—Shakespeare and Empire Day—or philosophically—Thomas Arnold and Karl Marx. This was a culture, a society, totally unprepared financially and especially psychologically for the economic catastrophe and emotional trauma which came with the end of the first World War.

The 1920s were difficult for Dowlais, although the heart of the town's economy was the steel works, many men were miners who travelled to nearby pits so the tumult of industrial unrest in that industry which climaxed in the General Strike was a constant weeping wound on the body of the community throughout the decade. Then in October 1930, with one sharp steel edged stroke the wound was opened wide and the life blood flooded out. In that

Cyfarthfa Band, about 1900, with Bandmaster, Livesey. Photo courtesy of Mr. & Mrs. Hugh Watkins.

Cyfarthfa Brass Band, 1905.

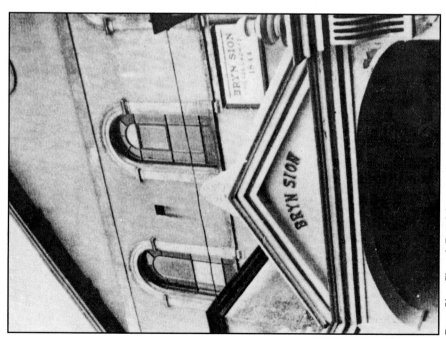

Bryn Sion Chapel, Dowlais.

Mounted on a special railway wagon, these two jet engines, of the type fitted to the Gloster Meteor record-breaking aircraft, were used last Thursday as an experiment in clearing the line at Cwmbargoed and Dowlais Top. Following the two-day blizzard this week, a great deal of work now awaits these jet engines, but it is understood that they are no longer at Cwmbargoed. R.A.F. personnel, including Flt. Lieut. W. E. Walton, D.F.C., operated the engines last week.

Throughout last week, workmen were hard at work clearing a snow drift which at one time nearly buried this L.M.S. engine at Penywern, Dowlais.

The Jet engines used to clear the snow at Cwmbargoed and Dowlais Top.

Sir Samuel Griffith, 1886. Photo courtesy of John Oxley Library, Queensland, 4101.

Sir Samuel Griffith. Photo courtesy of John Oxley Library, Queensland, 4101

Pengarnddu in its hey-day.

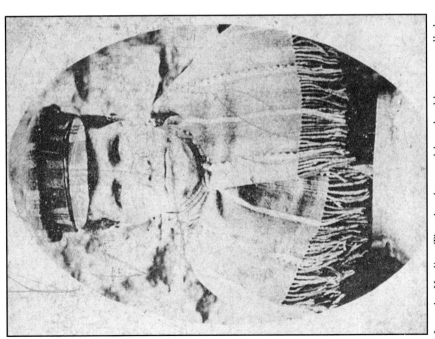

Jane the Haulier. The shawl around her shoulders was called a turnover.

Coal level where the "boys" worked.

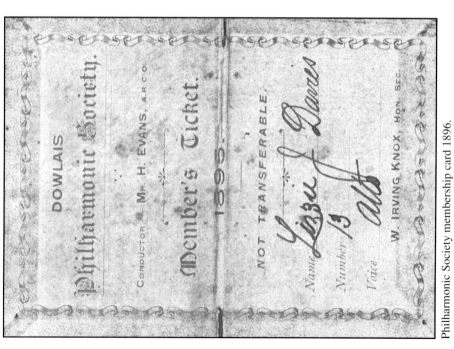

Philharmonic Society membership card 1896.

Morgan Morgan, later known as Morlais Morgan.

Evan Morgan with family.

Penywern Lane painted by Haydn Morgan.

Dowlais and Merthyr United Choir at the Queens Hall, London 1936. The mayor of Merthyr, Alderman Lewis Jones, with members of the Choir laid a wreath on the Cenotaph.

Penywern Chapel.

Ivor Street, Dowlais.

Chairs won at the Eisteddfodau during 1927 with four of the survivors. From left to right: Morlaisydd Morgan, John Rosser, John Morgan and Lew Pritchard.

Dowlais and Merthyr United Choir at the Queens Hall, London 1936.

The Last Book Performed—"Zurka The Gipsy Maid". Group taken in 1971. Back row (left to right): Nesta Evans, Barbara, Johnny Rosser (Barrack Row), Mr. Rosser (Blanche St.), Glenys, Unknown Rosser, Unknown, Llew Pritchard, Roy Richards, Lona Jones, Ann Jones (Cross Street). Centre row (left to right): Unknown, Howard Wilton, Ann Kinsey, Marion Davies, Unknown, Jean Davies, Margaret, Wendy Dean, Mary Evans, Betty Shankland, Kitty Jones, Josephine Harris Phelps, Shirley Jones, Linda Jones, Annette Strangewood, Glenys, Jennifer Davies,. Fairies (left to right): Linda Pritchard, Christine Jones, Glynis Jones, Linda Davies, Jeannie Arrianga, Laurie Jones, Ann Thomas, Margaret Collins, Elwyn Kinsey, Pam Smith, Roy Love, Unknown..

month the main part of the Dowlais Works closed and 3,000 men lost their jobs. Nothing would or could ever be the same again.

Perhaps a deliberate detachment from recent history of a cruel and unhappy period for so many led many local authorities in the 1950s and 1960s to adopt radical proposals for comprehensive redevelopment. The general opinion amongst building professionals and politicians in the 1950s and 1960s was that a "clean sweep" was best. The service infrastructure needed renewal, and new modern roads constructed. In the layout of houses and shops, pedestrians and cars should be separated. Modern methods of construction, particularly prefabrication, made it possible to build dwellings on a large scale at a lower cost, and in a shorter time. Renovation was not an option, certainly not one that was seriously considered, and in any case the available funds were for new houses, or more particularly flats. The die was cast. On the front page of the Merthyr Express of December 5th 1968, a headline read:

"Dowlais Chapel caught in the Pincers of Progress"

Mr. Bradley, Deputy Borough Engineer, had recommended to the Town Planning Sub-Committee that Bryn Seion Chapel be acquired. The Committee minutes read as follows:

"He stated that the chapel had been excluded from the Bryn Seion Street Compulsory Purchase Order for reasons determined by the Council, and it had now deteriorated to such an extent that the Chapel had been closed by the members who now use the Schoolroom for their services. He also stated that it is between the New Dowlais Redevelopment Area and the New shopping Centre and its continued existence would prevent the area being tidied up and redeveloped".

The houses in front of the chapel had been included in the Compulsory Purchase Order and had been demolished exposing the front of the chapel, including the covered entrance porch which stuck out absurdly, deprived of its physical and aesthetic support. Mr. Bradley went on to report, orally, that vandals had stripped lead from the chapel and water was seeping in. The Merthyr Express reported:

"Councillor J. Reddy told the Committee that the chapel people had been subject to shabby treatment. It was the only building in what was known as Bryn Seion Street, and for a year to eighteen months (the) congregation dressed in their Sunday best had been forced to walk through mud in order to reach their place of worship".

The minutes continue:

"The Deputy Borough Engineer reported that he had met Mr. Williams, Secretary of the Chapel, who advised the Deputy Borough Engineer that the chapel had held a meeting and had come to a decision that they could no longer carry on and were prepared to relinquish the premises to the Council".

Death is always ignominious; however, we may surround it by words and despite the whiteness of the shroud there is a blackness at its heart—the blackness of defeat. If this is true of individuals, it is even more true of societies, and there is nothing more demeaning than the death of a worshipping community. At the time of writing great concern is being expressed in the Western World at the destruction of hundreds of Romanian villages, as part of Policy of State Collectivisation. Scores of churches have been bulldozed, together with the medieval and post-medieval villages they served. In their place rise drab concrete blocks, bland, bleak and uniform. The policy is described by others as "Stalinist", apparently the Rumanian Government does not regard that adjective as necessarily unflattering, in any case the programme of destruction continues.

Unfortunately in the British Isles there are many similar examples of needless demolition—who are we to cast the first stone? The Euston Propylaeum, the original Bank of England, the Friary in Cardiff, and nearer to home The Triangle, Dowlais Stables, Gwernllwyn Chapel—miserably commemorated in the name of a block of flats—all destroyed for no reason at all. The only excuse was ignorance and that is surely the most degrading excuse of all. At the end of the list, the long melancholy list, Bryn Seion Chapel 1844–1969. As the bulldozer tore up those "tacelated tiles" whose conscience stirred?

References

The majority of this essay is taken from "Hanes Eglwys Bryn Seion, Dowlais 1832–1907" by Isaac Jones, Tonypandy 1907.

Other references include:

"Hanes Eglwys Annibynol Bethania Dowlais" by William Griffiths, Dowlais 1898.

"Hanes Eglwys Crist yn Zoar, Merthyr", by Rev. R. Griffiths, Tabor, Merthyr Tydfil, 1869.

"The History of the Hen Dy Cwrdd, Cefn Coed y Cymer", by Tom Lewis, Llandysul 1947.

Merthyr Tydfil:
The Development of an Urban Community

by JOSEPH GROSS

In mediaeval times, Merthyr Tydfil was part of the Lordship of Senghenydd, in the Hundred of Upper Senghenydd. It became a parish at the time of the Norman Conquest of Glamorgan in the 13th century. In fact the earliest written evidence of the church in Merthyr dates to 1254, to a Valour ecclesiasticus, a valuation of church property of that year. When Gilbert de Clare built the castle of Caerphilly, it became the centre of administration from which Merthyr was ruled. The Castle was the place where the Sheriff of Glamorgan had his Court and later a Constable of Senghenydd was appointed to act as his deputy. By 1540 there were 80 landholders in Uwch Caiach who paid rent directly to the Lords of Glamorgan. They in turn had smaller subtenants.

By the middle of the 17th century there was a High Constable of Caerphilly Higher, a post that existed until 1908 and in later years was filled by people from Merthyr. The Parish was administered by a Vestry, consisting of the Rector, two churchwardens, a parish or vestry clerk, 4 overseers of the poor and surveyors in each of the five hamlets of which the parish consisted, namely Garth, Gellideg, Heol Wermwd, Taff and Cynon and Forest. The overseers of the poor were appointed by the Justices of the Peace. These Justices were elected by the Sheriff from the local gentry and large shareholders. The duty of the Vestry was to raise a quarterly rate and use it for the support of the poor. As to Parliamentary representation, there were two members for Glamorgan, one representing the Borough, the other the County. Merthyr formed part of the County electorate. There were some 1,500-2,000 electors in the County during the 18th century. The members of Parliament were all connected with the great ruling families of landowners and aristocrats. From 1790-1807 for instance the County Member was Thomas Wyndham of Dunraven Castle, one of the greatest landowners in Glamorgan.

Early in the 19th century Petty Sessions were introduced to deal with common crimes such as drunkenness and petty thieving. The first such Court of Justices for Caerphilly Higher, i.e. the Merthyr Parish, was held at the Star Inn.

The population of Merthyr by about 1700 numbered some 700. They consisted of landowners, farmers and rural craftsmen, such as smiths, wheelwrights, corn and cloth millers. Yet it would be wrong to underrate the very considerable intellectual activity going on in Merthyr in the first half of the 17th century. From the earliest days of Nonconformity Merthyr was one of the principal centres of Dissent in Glamorgan. The first meetings took place in the farm house in Blaencanaid north of Merthyr, from about 1640. The Merthyr Nonconformists had strong links with the church in Llanigon in Breconshire. In the second half of the century the denominations represented were Independents, Presbyterians and Baptists, soon followed by Quakers. Thomas Erbury, who in 1630 owned a forge in Pontygwaith and a furnace in Pontyrhun, was a Quaker. Another Quaker, Mary Chapman, left a plot of land for a burial ground to the Quakers. It was situated to the south of the parish and became known as Quakers Yard. After the restoration of Charles II the Dissenters suffered prosecution but they clung courageously to their beliefs. Vavassour Powell, a famous Puritan, was arrested whilst preaching in Merthyr and taken to Cardiff jail. In 1689 the Toleration Act was passed and shortly afterwards the Dissenters built their first church in Cwm y Glo. Worship continued there till 1749. Before that, in 1747, the Armenians among the Congregation broke away and founded a church in Cefn Coed, Hen Dy Cûrdd. The remaining Independents in Cwm y Glo moved to Ynysgau in 1749. The Baptists founded their first church in Zion in Twyn y Rodyn in 1788.

Thus we see that by the middle of the 18th century there was a well established number of Dissenters in Merthyr who set great store by intellectual understanding, theological knowledge and religious truth. In this rural community with its strong religious beliefs now arose forces of world wide importance, namely the Industrial Revolution.

In the area between Merthyr and Cardiff lies the South Wales coalfield and the minerals of coal, ironstone and limestone all are found near the surface near Merthyr. These minerals are crucial for the making of iron. They had been exploited by the local inhabitants on a small scale for many years and ironmaking in small furnaces had been carried out since the 15th century. The extraction of the above mentioned minerals on a large scale for the making of iron became lucrative with the invention and improvement of the method of smelting of iron with the aid of coke instead of charcoal, a process invented by the Darbys of Coalbrookdale. Capitalists were now attracted to the Merthyr area. The first development took place in Dowlais, where a partnership of entrepreneurs obtained a lease in 1759 from Alice Lady Windsor to erect a furnace. Among the partners were Thomas Lewis of Llanishen and Isaac Wilkinson from Denbigshire and five others. Isaac Wilkinson sold his share in the furnace in 1762 and a year later joined John Guest from Broseley in Shropshire in obtaining a lease from the Earl of Plymouth for land to erect a furnace to the South of Merthyr. This was called the Plymouth furnace. The Plymouth furnace was not successful and was sold in 1766 to Anthony Bacon, who rebuilt it. John Guest then became manager of the Dowlais furnace in 1767. Here there was greater success and John Guest became a partner in 1782. He was succeeded as manager by his son Thomas, who remained in charge in Dowlais from 1785 to 1807. Three blast furnaces operated in 1800. Thomas Guest was succeeded by his son John Josiah Guest, who developed the works so that they became the largest in the town at the time of his death in 1852. Sir John Josiah was knighted in 1831 and later married Lady Charlotte. She was a very talented Lady who learned Welsh and translated the Mabinogion into English.

To return to the Plymouth Works, these as we said were acquired in 1766 by Anthony Bacon and were managed for him by his brother in law Richard Hill. Richard Hill obtained the lease of the works in 1786. He died in 1806 and was succeeded by his three sons, of whom the youngest, Anthony eventually became sole proprietor. There were three blast furnaces in Plymouth in 1806.

The third iron works were the Cyfarthfa Works, founded by Anthony Bacon in 1765. The land was leased from Lord Talbot of Hensol Castle and Mr. Michael Richards of Cardiff. The works engineer was Charles Wood, who left a valuable diary of the first two years of the works. The first blast furnace was erected in 1767. In 1773 Anthony Bacon built a mill for boring cannon. Bacon took as partner in 1777 a London merchant, Richard Crawshay. Another ironmaster who was to become prominent in Merthyr was Francis Homfray, owner of a furnace in Broseley, who came to Merthyr in 1783 to lease Anthony Bacon's cannon mill. He worked it for one year only and the mill was then leased to Richard Crawshay. When Bacon died in 1786, Richard Crawshay obtained the management of both mill and furnace, and he eventually became sole owner of the Cyfarthfa Works. Richard Crawshay developed the works with great success, particularly after he obtained the rights to use the puddling process developed by Henry Cort and patented in 1784. Henry Cort's invention was a process of converting pig iron into wrought iron by the use of coal instead of charcoal used until that time. First the adoption of the puddling process in Cyfarthfa proved difficult. This induced Richard Crawshay to take up residence in Merthyr in 1791 and to assume the management of the works himself. He overcame the initial teething troubles of the puddling process. He was so successful that he not only acquired a large fortune but also established a lead over the other ironmasters in Merthyr. His works by the early 1820's had become the largest in Merthyr and the world. It was only after Richard Crawshays death in 1810 and the succession of John Josiah Guest to the Dowlais Works that the latter overtook the Cyfarthfa Works. There were three blast furnaces in Cyfarthfa in 1796 and six in 1803, when over 2,000 people were employed. Richard Crawshay died in 1810 and left a fortune of over 1½ million pounds.

The fourth and last of the ironworks founded in Merthyr was the Penydarren Works, founded in 1784 by Francis Homfray. We met him already when he operated the cannon mill in Cyfarthfa. He left these works to start works of his own in Merthyr. He was assisted by his three sons Jeremiah, Thomas and Samuel and George Foreman. The works were completed in 1786. Samuel Homfray eventually became senior partner. He built the first of the great mansions of the ironmasters, Penydarren House, with extensive grounds and hot houses, where he grew tropical fruit and flowers. The works gave their name to the Penydarren Tramroad, to be discussed presently.

The products of the iron works in the first place were pig iron. This could be used in castings or converted into wrought iron by reheating and consolidation in the puddling process, followed by hammering and rolling. Very large items of cast iron have survived e.g. in sections of river and canal bridges, and in lintels and other items embedded in masonry. The wrought iron was worked into bar iron. Bar iron output in Cyfarthfa increased between 1790 and 1798 from about 2,300 tons to about 6,000 tons due to the puddling process. Output of all works increased dramatically from 1830 onwards with the production of rails for the new railways. This became the chief output of the Merthyr ironworks to all parts of the world. The output shipped on the Glamorganshire Canal from all four ironworks increased from 40,000 tons in 1817 to 70,000 in 1830. The total number of blast furnaces in Merthyr in 1824 was 31.

One of the difficulties facing the ironmasters coming to Merthyr to exploit the mineral resources was the problem of transport. As the river Taff is not navigable, the only means of access to the hilly upland of Glamorgan was by trackroads leading over the mountain from Cardiff to Caerphilly and to Merthyr. So all goods had to be transported by pack animals, horses, mules, donkeys. Soon after coming to Merthyr, Anthony Bacon persuaded the landowners and farmers of the area to contribute to the construction of a road in the valley of the Taff to Cardiff. This road was built and later upgraded to a turnpike road and extended to Brecon. Now carriages and horsedrawn waggons could travel to Cardiff. However as the four ironworks increased their output further improvements of the transport system became necessary and in 1794 the Glamorganshire Canal was opened between Merthyr and Cardiff, one of the technical achievements of the time. Transport of goods and materials within the works and from the mines and quarries to the works was carried on so called tramroads. These consisted of cast iron rails fastened to stone sleepers on which waggons called trams travelled drawn by horses. One such tramroad became particularly important. It was the Penydarren Tramroad which served three of the Merthyr ironworks in conveying goods from Merthyr to a depot on the Glamorganshire Canal, Abercynon, 7½ miles from Merthyr. This tramroad was built to alleviate the congestion on a section of the canal between Merthyr and Abercynon. Goods were taken on the Tram-road to Abercynon and there transferred to barges to take them by canal to Cardiff. The Penydarren Tramroad became famous in 1804 when a steam engine designed by Richard Trevithick driven by its own steam pulled a train of trams and a load of 70 tons from Merthyr to Abercanaid, thus becoming the first locomotive. It preceded Stephenson's Rocket by many years but Trevithick's invention was not exploited commercially.

The development of the Railways following Stephenson's Rocket had an enormous importance for the Merthyr ironworks. As mentioned, from the 1830's onwards the principal products of the ironworks were rails and other railway furniture. The first railway built to reach Merthyr from Cardiff was the Taff Railway opened in 1841. Several other railway lines were built to Merthyr in later years, competing for the lucrative transport of first iron and steel, and later coal.

The increase in industrial activity required a large increase in the work force and thus of the population as a whole. The number of inhabitants rose dramatically from about 700 in 1770 to 7,700 in 1801, 22,000 in 1831 and 46,000 in 1851. This increase meant a constant influx of people from outside of Merthyr. They came from all parts of Wales, from England and Ireland. They left an often precarious living on the land for regular and better paid employment in the ironworks.

Each of the four works formed a distinct community depending on the patriarchal rule of the ironmasters. The master had to provide many of the amenities and services which in other places would have been supplied by a well ordered local authority. The master appointed the works doctors and established surgeries, built some of the dwellings for his workers, although most were provided by speculative builders. Some works provided truck shops, e.g. the Guests and Homfrays, although the Crawshays did not. Later in the 19th century the masters provided works schools for the children of their employees, particularly the Dowlais Schools developed under the guidance of Lady Charlotte Guest. The ironmasters supported churches and chapels.

In the early years of the works the masters lived near their works and built themselves large, luxurious mansions. The pattern was set by Samuel Homfray who lived in considerable style in Penydarren House. This was followed by William Crawshay II who built the large pseudogothic Cyfarthfa Castle. The Guests were comparatively modest. Dowlais House never displayed vulgar ostentation. Anthony Hill too only built the large Pentrebach House two years before his death.

The growth of the ironworks led to the development of a thriving self confident middle class. It consisted of the officials of the ironworks, the doctors, lawyers and preachers, and an increasing number of prosperous shopkeepers. They were the regular leaders of the Vestry except in times of economic crisis. The members of the middle class formed the Cyfarthfa Philosophical Society which met in the Dynevor Arms in Georgetown. They were the leading members of the various chapels and gradually exercised political power as supporters of the Radical Movement. Prominent among them was William Meyrick a very successful lawyer, attorney to the Crawshays and the Glamorganshire Canal Company. Others were the influential James family. The way in which they gained influence is interesting. We showed earlier that at the end of the 18th century the administration of the Parish was in the hands of the vestry. This consisted of the Rector, 2 Churchwardens, the Parish Clerk and 4 Overseers of the Poor. Their main task was the support of the poor inhabitants. The vestry determined the poor rate to be levied each quarter. It was levied on the ironmasters according to the number of furnaces in blast, and on all householders. The ironmasters did not usually attend the vestry except in times of crises, when the Poor Rate rose alarmingly. Then they stepped in, took over the parish and introduced administrative reforms. Such a crisis occurred in 1811 and again in 1816. On these occasions the poor rate rose to alarming levels, a committee of townspeople failed to cope and the ironmasters intervened and designed schemes for administrative improvements. These schemes were carried out by a small group of merchants, solicitors and shopkeepers of the town. These men thus gained political influence. In 1822 an important change occurred. A select Vestry was created, where a small committee of Parish Members were elected to make decisions on behalf of the rest of the parishioners. Every April the parish elected two churchwardens, four overseers and 20 select Vestry men. These were the new government of the town until the coming of the Board of Guardians in 1836. The ironmasters ceased to attend after one year and the Vestry was then run by the middle class members. Another important step was the appointment of a Stpendiary Magistrate in 1829. He was a paid judge in contrast to the unpaid Justices of the Peace. Earlier, in 1809, the Court of Requests had been created, which dealt with small debts and was intended to protect the shopkeepers of the town.

We must now turn to the group of people who are the real unsung heroes of the industrial revolution, the workers. Employment in the works, mines and collieries was nasty and brutal. Most of the processes required hard physical effort and were carried out in circumstances of heat, noise and great physical danger. Women and young children were employed. Accidents were frequent, medical assistance primitive, insurance unheard of. The living conditions of the workers were often poor.

The houses were built solidly enough of stone, and after the opening of the Glamorganshire Canal in 1794, usually covered with slate. But they were constructed without any regard to neighbouring property and without street plans. They were often packed closely together in small courts and narrow alley ways. Many were built back to back; many people lived in cellar dwellings. Very few had toilets. There was a total lack of sewers and surface drainage. All slops and refuse were thrown into the streets. These were in wet weather often impassable for mud.

The worst evil however was the total lack of an adequate provision of water. The water in the principal streams was diverted and used in the ironworks. The surface of the mountains surrounding the town was carefully drained and the water collected in large ponds and reservoirs for exclusive use in the ironworks. After passing through the works the water was so contaminated that it was no longer usable for domestic purposes. The only supply available to the population were a few private wells and a small number of water spouts for general use. Thus there was a chronic shortage of pure water for the majority of the people.

As a consequence the health of the people suffered. Particularly appaling was the death rate of children. Out of 1,000 children born in 1850, over 180 died in their first year, 15 times as many as today. The average age of death in 1851 was 17½ years. In 1976 it was 71 years. Illness and deaths were often caused by epidemics. The most dreaded were the occurrences of cholera. The first time it struck was in 1832/3 when 160 persons died. Next in 1849 the number of deaths was 1432. Two more outbreaks in 1854 and 1866 claimed 424 and 119 persons respectively. Children suffered particularly from infectious diseases: small pox, scarlet fever, tuberculosis. Pneumonia, bronchitis and dysentery were prevalent.

Yet it must not be overlooked that the workers were comparatively well off economically, even though they were subject to the periodic depressions of the iron industry. Many travellers describe with astonishment the good furniture one could see in the houses, the dressers with glass and china, shining tin and copper utensils, Eight Day clocks.

Naturally the growing prosperity of the town attracted its share of undesirable elements, thieves, pick pockets, vagrants, prostitutes. They congregated in the notorious districts of Chinatown and the Cellars. The socalled Nymphs of Pontstore house were known for their good looks. The greatest bully in Chinatown was known as the Emperor. The Parish constables could not cope with this unruly crowd and a regular police force was at last created in 1841 when 12 men of the Glamorgan County Police force were stationed here.

During the first quarter of the nineteenth century several slumps in the economic fortunes of the iron industry occurred which sometimes led to riots. The worst occurred in 1831. The causes leading up to it were several. There was first the question of religion. We have discussed the growing influence of Nonconformity. 23 meeting places were registered between 1797 and 1836. The Unitarians became politically influential and supported Radicalism. Leading the movement were members of the rising middle classes. Radicals wanted universal suffrage. They opposed the Corn Laws which imposed import duties on grain and thus kept the price of bread high. The movement spread to the working classes who became accustomed to hear and debate arguments concerning political rights and reform and the nature of a just society. Their increasing self confidence led to demands for the right to form unions.

In this atmosphere of growing political awareness occurred one of the periodical depressions which hit the iron industry. Even the radical William Crawshay II was forced to cut wages in 1831. Workers became unemployed and got into debt. The shopkeepers became desperate and the Court of Requests ruthlessly collected debts and seized the property of the poor. In this atmosphere the Reform Bill was published, in March 1831. Public meetings in Merthyr as in other parts of the country were held in an atmosphere of great excitement. William Crawshay rallied his workmen and helped them to draft a petition for Parliamentary Reform.

It was this which probably unleashed the pentup forces of working class power. On May 9 crowds paraded in Merthyr demonstrating for Reform. Windows of known opponents of the Bill were broken. Two men were brought before the Magistrates and were rescued by the crowd. Public order broke down. On May 15th large crowds marched to the Waun Fair carrying a banner inscribed "Reform". However the speeches were mainly concerned with a demand for the abolition of the Court of Requests and the imprisonment for debt. On May 23 William Crawshay dismissed 84 puddlers. This was probably the signal for the ensuing violence. On June 1, over 100 houses in Merthyr and Cefn Coed were visited by rioters. Coffins house, where the Court of Requests was held was ransacked, goods stored there, which had been seized for debts, were returned to their owners and papers and books found burned.

On the next day 80 soldiers from Brecon occupied the Castle Inn. They were attacked by a crowd of some 7,000 to 10,000 people. In the Castle Inn were the High Sheriff of Glamorgan, the Merthyr Magistrates and three of the four ironmasters. The leaders of the crowd were Lewis Lewis the Huntsman and Richard Lewis, Dick Penderyn. The Riot Act was read. The crowd attacked and disarmed several soldiers. The troops opened fire and killed or wounded several people. The number killed is not known, possibly two dozen. The crowd dispersed. The insurgents moved to Cefn Coed. They ambushed 34 men of the Swansea Yeomanry who had come from Hirwaun and disarmed them. Another military contingent, 40 men of the Merthyr garrison who had gone to Brecon for ammunition, were attacked on their way back to Merthyr near Cefn Coed and had to turn back. A few days later 12,000-15,000 men from Monmouthshire marched to Merthyr. They were met at Dowlais Top by soldiers. John J. Guest read the Riot Act and the men turned back. That was the end of the rising. Resistance ceased on June 6th. Several leaders of the riot were arrested. At the trial two men were condemned to death. One was Lewis

Lewis the Huntsman who was later reprieved and deported. The other, Richard Lewis, Dick Penderyn, was hanged in Cardiff jail on 13th August 1831. He has become a legendary figure, a martyr of the early working class movement. A plaque to his memory at the Merthyr Public Library was unveiled in 1977 by Len Murray, the then General Secretary of the Trades Union Congress.

As a result of the rising, the Whig Government made Merthyr (with Aberdare) into an electoral constituency in the Reform Act of 1832. John J. Guest was returned unopposed as the first Member of Parliament for Merthyr. His election was due to the support of the radical Non-conformist group led by D. W. James, who wielded great influence in the new electorate of some 500 middle class voters who had obtained the right to vote under the Reform Act.

Yet important as the influence of the radical group was, it could be overruled by the power of the ironmasters, particularly the Crawshays and the Hills. One glaring example was their power to obstruct the adoption of the Municipal Corporation Act of 1834. This Act enabled large industrial towns which lacked the status of a chartered town to obtain such a charter. Several towns in Wales and England enjoyed charters since mediaeval times. On the other hand the new industrial towns, such as Merthyr, were still administered as Parish Vestries. The Charter under the Act of 1834 conferred powers of full independence of local self government. Many industrial towns obtained the charter at the time e.g. Manchester, Leeds and Birmingham. In Merthyr too a petition for Incorporation was discussed at a public meeting held in 1837. Yet although several ironmasters among others declared their support in public, the petition was never presented to the Privy Council. H. W. Southey, the proprietor of the Merthyr Express writing many years later, gives the following explanation: "Most likely the ironmasters or the majority of them, saw that paternal government which clothed them with supreme power in parochial affairs could not possibly be maintained under a municipality and they had merely to cause it to be known that they regarded a movement of this nature with disfavour to deter the bulk of the residents from proceeding in opposition to their wishes." Further resolutions for incorporation in 1857, 1874/6 and 1898 were similarly frustrated and it was not until 1903 that the Charter was obtained. It is interesting to speculate which local services could have been obtained or obtained much sooner if Incorporation had been achieved at the first attempt. Probably the water supply could have been obtained 20 years earlier than actually achieved, a sewerage system 30 years earlier. A Town Hall, public parks, closer control of buildings and alignment and the cleaning of streets could all have been achieved much sooner.

The next important step in the development of local government occurred in 1834 with the passing of the new Poor Law Act. Adjacent parishes were allowed to group themselves into Unions for the purpose of relieving the poor. In 1836 the Merthyr Tydfil Union was formed comprising originally 8 parishes. In 1863 the number was reduced to five. The administration of the Union was in the hands of the Board of Guardians, chosen by the electorate of the parishes of the Union. This Board was to become practically the local government until the establishment of the Merthyr Board of Health, replacing to a large extent the powers of the Select Vestry.

The duty of the Board of Guardians was the relief of the poor, the socalled paupers. Relieving officers were appointed to carry out this duty. They were paid full time officials, whereas the Guardians performed their tasks as voluntary workers. Relief was of two kinds. Outdoor relief consisted of payments in cash or grants of food, clothing and medicine. Indoor relief consisted in accommodation in a special building, the Workhouse. There shelter, food and medical care were provided. The poor law in general and the workhouse in particular were dreaded by the poor from the very beginning because of the harsh principle applied of "Less eligibility", namely that relief offered should only allow a standard of living below that of the lowest paid employed person to encourage people to seek paid employment. In Merthyr a Work House was not built until 1853. The Board of Guardians was abolished in 1929, the Poor Law in 1948. One of the duties of the Guardians was the care of the sick poor. As early as 1836 a medical officer was appointed. In 1846 the Board of Guardians became responsible for the removal of nuisances such as refuse deposited in the streets and houses. Inspectors of Nuisances were appointed to carry out this task. The Guardians were responsible to take measures to combat the cholera epidemic which occurred in 1849. Nine extra Medical Officers of Health were appointed, assisted by a lay visitor each. There was no hospital in Merthyr at that time where the victims of the disease could be treated. A House of Refuge was built to receive up to 100 still healthy persons from houses affected by the disease. A new burial ground in Pant was opened, as the existing burial grounds could not cope with the interment of the 1432 victims which the cholera claimed.

In 1853 the Workhouse was built with an Infirmary within its grounds. A House Surgeon was appointed for the Infirmary, and a Master and Matron were in charge of the Workhouse. During the third cholera epidemic in 1854 another House of Refuge was build, a solid brick structure off the Brecon Road. It later became a Fever Hospital of the Board of Health. The Infirmary at the Workhouse was enlarged in 1867, 1897 and in the present century. Today St. Tydfil's Hospital has taken over all buildings of the old Workhouse and later additions.

Public administration took a decisive step forward when the Merthyr Tydfil Local Board of Health was established. Before the Board could be set up, a public enquiry had to be conducted. This was held in 1849 by T. W. Rammell. Mr. Rammell issued a now famous report in 1850. In it he describes the atrocious living conditions of the vast majority of the people of Merthyr: the poor housing, the lack of a supply of good drinking water, the absence of drains and sewers, the inadequate layout of houses and streets. The report then showed how these deplorable conditions adversely affected the health of the population, resulting in diseases and epidemics.

With this evidence before him, Rammell had no difficulty in recommending that a Local Board of Health should be set up and this was done in 1850. It consisted of 14 elected members with Sir John Josiah Guest as Chairman. Other members of the Board included Henry Austin Bruce, Anthony Hill, Robert Thompson Crawshay, and William Meyrick. The main duties of the Board were to carry out essential drainage, to lay down a sewerage system and to provide an adequate supply of water. The Board were responsible for street cleaning, paving and lighting. They were empowered to register and inspect slaughter houses and common lodging houses, to ensure that no cellar dwellings be let or built. They could provide public leisure grounds and parks.

The Board appointed a Clerk and Surveyor and an Inspector of Nuisances by 1851. Fifty gas lamps for street lighting were installed in 1850. A temporary Medical Officer of Health was appointed in 1853, a permanent one in 1865. This was the eminent Dr. T. J. Dyke. A long delay occurred in one of the most important tasks of the Board, the provision of a water supply. An Act of Parliament was obtained in 1852. This was allowed to lapse due to the opposition of the so called riparian owners, namely the owners of a large section of the river Taff. They were the Crawshays, the Hills and the Glamorganshire Canal Company. They feared a possible loss of the water supply to their works and also an increase in the rates. A new Act was obtained in 1858, largely due to the energy and diplomacy of G. T. Clarke, the resident Trustee of the Dowlais Iron Works since 1856 and Chairman of the Board of Health since 1857. Water reached Merthyr in 1861. An impounding reservoir was built in 1862. The sewerage system was started in 1864 and the untreated effluent discharged into the river Taff from 1868. This met with opposition from another local industrialist, this time an important coal owner, John Nixon. He had begun sinking a shaft for a coal mine in Merthyr Vale in 1869. Later in that year he obtained an injunction against the Merthyr Board of Health on the grounds that sewage in the Taff was obnoxious to his workers and horses working in the preparation of the pits in Merthyr Vale. The injunction prevented the Board of Health from connecting further houses to the sewer but allowed present sewerage to flow into the Taff on condition that a treatment plant be constructed. The Board of Health eventually commissioned the building of a treatment plant in Troedyrhiw. It was of a— for the time-highly advanced design called "The downward intermittent filtration system". Sewage was let to flow over a plot of land and filtered through a system of underground pipes. It emerged as clear water. The plant was known as the sewage farm. It was completed in 1872 and later extended, as the population increased. Eventually the Merthyr and Aberdare Boards of Health joined forces and formed a Joint Farm Management Committee to administer the sewage disposal of both towns.

It is interesting to note that John Nixon organised another attack on the Merthyr Board of Health at the same time. He induced 77 rate payers living in Merthyr Vale to apply to the General Board of Health in London for the separation of the Merthyr Vale area from the area of the Merthyr Board of Health and the establishment of a separate Board of Health in Merthyr Vale. The Inspector appointed to hold a public enquiry recommended rejection of the application. He pointed out that the enquiry was exclusively in the interest of Messrs. Nixon, Cory and Taylor, the proprietors of the new coal mine. He also stated that the new water supply would greatly benefit the people of Merthyr Vale.

As the years passed, the population of Merthyr increased. It reached 46.000 in 1861 and 58.500 by 1891. The increase occurred not only in the northern section of the parish but also in the south, where new villages and townships developed: Pentrebach, Troedyrhiw, Merthyr Vale, Edwardsville, Trebarris and Quakers Yard. This required a continuous extension of the water supply and sewerage. New Sewage farms were created in Cilfynydd and new water reservoirs were built on the Taf Fechan River below the Brecon Beacons, the Lower and Upper Neuadd Reservoirs.

The fight against infectious diseases continued under the Medical Officer for Health, Dr. T. J. Dyke, who remained in office until his death in 1908. He issued a series of admirable Annual Medical Reports, models of their kind in interest and lucidity. He enjoyed a European reputation. During his term of office the death rate fell from 33 to 23 per 1000 of the population and that of tuberculosis from 38 to 18 per 10.000. After 1864 no further outbreaks of cholera occurred. The main diseases of the period were small pox, diphtheria, scarlet fever and the scourge of tuberculosis, not conquered until the first half of this century.

The duties of the Board of Health expanded. They gradually included the paving, making and channelling of streets, the making of roads and bridges. Housing exercised the attention of the Board in increasing measure. By 1860 building plans for dwellings had to be submitted to the Board for approval. By 1880 the Board had powers to declare substandard premises to be unfit for human habitation. The Board were responsible for fire fighting, which in Merthyr was carried out by the local police until World War Two.

The Local Board of Health ceased to exist on 31.12.1894 when its duties were taken over by the Merthyr District Council. By then the franchise had been substantially expanded and the working classes now became the dominant factor in local politics. Since 1831 Liberalism had been the most influential power, although Merthyr remained a centre of Chartism, even if the people of Merthyr did not participate in the march on Newport. Yet the influence of the Chapel remained strong. Sir John J. Guest retained his seat as M.P. for Merthyr until his death in 1852. He was succeeded by Henry Austin Bruce one of the Trustees of the Dowlais Ironworks, till 1868. The Reform Act of 1867 made Merthyr into a two member constituency and increased the number of voters to 14.000. The developing independence of thought of the working classes and the radicalism of the chapels led in 1868 to the election of Henry Richards, the socalled Apostle of Peace. It was a sensational result. Here was a man without wealth, without the support of the local ironmasters, a Nonconformist, who defeated the powerful nominee of the local industrial magnates. The second member to be elected was Richard Fothergill, a rich industrialist. Officially they were members of the Liberal Party, as were all M.P.s until Keir Hardie. Henry Richards retained his seat until his death in 1888, when he was succeeded by W. Pritchard Morgan. Morgan retained his seat until 1900. Richard Fothergill was succeeded in 1880 by Charles Herbert James, a member of the influential James family of Merthyr. He remained M.P. until 1888. His place was taken by another powerful industrialist, David Alfred Thomas, who retained his seat until 1906.

In the second half of the 19th century important changes took place in the local industry. The old iron industry declined in importance. The Penydarren Works ceased to produce iron in 1858 due to managerial incompetence. Ironmaking in Plymouth works ceased after the death of Anthony Hill in 1862 and the new owners concentrated their activities on coal mining. By this time a revolutionary process of making mild steel had been developed by Bessemer in a converter named after him. The Dowlais Works were the first to adopt this process and the works continued to prosper. By this time the local iron stone proved to be no longer economical and iron ore had to be imported from other parts of the country and from abroad, especially from Spain. This meant that all the ore had to be brought to Merthyr by rail, from the coast at Cardiff and this added considerably to the cost of production. This led to the establishing of new steel works by the Dowlais Company at the coast in Cardiff. In this crucial period for the iron industry, the Cyfarthfa Works suffered a serious setback. In 1874 a serious strike occurred in all the works in Merthyr. Robert Thompson Crawshay refused to negotiate with the striking workers and the works were closed during the years 1874-1879. They were only re-opened after Robert Thompson Crawshays death and the heirs spent a large sum of money in converting the works to steel production. However they were not able to compete with the Dowlais Works. Eventually the Cyfarthfa Works were sold to the proprietors of the Dowlais Works, the firm of Guest Keen and Nettlefolds, who acquired Dowlais works in 1901. The sale of the Cyfarthfa Works occurred in 1902. Steelmaking in Cyfarthfa slowly petered out, was resumed to a limited extent during the 1914-18 war, when the works finally closed. However the coal resources of the old ironworks were now exploited for sale. The coal industry steadily increased and new pits were sunk in Merthyr Vale, Treharris and Bedlinog. The steady increase of the work force in the mines led to a growing influence of the coalminers and their unions. The Miners Federation of South Wales was founded in 1898.The Working Class was now able to exercise increasing political power. This was made possible through the continuing extension of the franchise and the important reform of Local Government. The County Council Act of 1888 was of immense importance for the reform of local government. It destroyed the political authority wielded by the gentry through their monopoly of the magisterial system and made it possible for men from lower social classes to share in government. In 1894 the Parish Council Act introduced local government into the parishes and the old urban and rural sanitary authorities were reconstructed as urban and rural District Councils.

Thus the Local Merthyr Board of Health was abolished and its functions were taken over by the Merthyr Tydfil Urban District Council from 1.1.1895. It had 18 elected members. All elections were by universal ballot of rate paying male inhabitants. The working classes now organised themselves for political action. An Independent Labour Party Branch was formed in Merthyr in 1895 and a Trades Council in 1909. A Labour Conference in Abernant adopted Keir Hardie as Parliamentary candidate for Merthyr for the 1900 elections. He won the second seat, becoming the Junior Member for Merthyr. D. L. Thomas retained his seat as Senior Member.

The final development of Merthyr as an Urban Community occurred with the granting of the Charter of Incorporation. After many failed attempts a petition was again presented in 1903 to the Privy Council. This was opposed by the Railway Companies, the Merthyr Vale and Treharris Collieries and Cardiff Corporation. Yet the Charter was granted in 1905. This created the Municipal Borough of Merthyr Tydfil. It had a Council of 32 members, including the Mayor and eight aldermen. Goscombe John, R.A. designed the coat of arms and D. A. Thomas donated a beautiful gold chain for the Mayor. The first election of 1905 was a victory for the Labour Party. It was a complete defeat of the Liberal Nonconformist organisation of the town. Of the 32 members 14 belonged to the Labour Party. The new Mayor, Enoch Morrell, was a checkweigher from Troedyrhiw and one of the founders of the Merthyr Labour Party.

In 1908 a further change of status of the Council occurred, when Merthyr became a Municipal County Borough. It now obtained its own Police Force, under a Chief Constable, its own Commission of the Peace and Court of Quarter Sessions. The new status also conferred powers to control secondary education in the Borough.

In this article we traced the development of the local administration of Merthyr from its beginnings as a rural parish at the end of the eighteenth century, when it was administered by a Parish Vestry, which later became a Select Vestry. Later important community functions were taken over first by the Board of Guardians and later by the Local Board of Health. Local Government as we know it came when the Urban District Council was created in 1895. Merthyr obtained its Charter and became a Municipal Borough in 1905. Finally it achieved the status of a Municipal County Borough in 1908.

References

1. John Addis: The Crawshay Dynasty. The University of Wales Press 1957.
2. T.V. Davies: Farms and Farmers of Senghenydd Sypra prior to the Industrial Revolution. Private Edition 1992.
3. Glamorgan County History. Volume V. Industrial Glamorgan. Editor Glanmor Williams.
4. Joseph Gross. A Brief History of Merthyr Tydfil. Starling Press 1980 .
5. Edgar Jones. A History of G.K.N. Volume I. Macmillans 1987.
6. Merthyr Tydfil Parish Minute Book.
7. Merthyr Tydfil Board of Guardians. Minutes 1836-1929.
8. Merthyr Tydfil Board of Health. Minutes 1850-1894.
9. Merthyr Tydfil Urban District Council Minutes 1895-1905.
10. Merthyr Tydfil Municipal Borough Minutes 1905-1908
11. Merthyr Tydfil County Borough Minutes 1908-1974.
12. Merthyr Telegraph 1855-1881.
13. John Owen. A Short History of the Dowlais Ironworks Merthyr Tydfil Borough Corporation 1972.
14. Charles Wilkins. The History of Merthyr Tydfil 1st edition 1867 2nd edition 1908.
15. Glanmor Williams. The Earliest Nonconformists in Merthyr Tydfil. Merthyr Historian Volume One. Ed. J. Gross . 1976.
16. Gwyn A. Williams. The Merthyr Rising. Croom Helm 1978.

Winter,
Nineteen Forty Seven

by JOSH POWELL

In most parts of the British Isles, the weather is a favourite topic of conversation—Merthyr Tydfil is no exception.

One might say, "We get an awful lot of weather in Merthyr."

Another agrees, "In Merthyr we can get a year's weather in a day."

A third adds, "If our visitors don't like our weather, tell them to hang around for a few hours."

These comments illustrate the changeable nature of the weather in Merthyr Tydfil. With the exception of sandstorms and duststorms, local people can expect a taste of every category of the earth's weather as classified by the Meteorological Office. Oftimes these changes occur with remarkable rapidity.

Therefore, it is hardly surprising that our weather rarely merits any historical significance. Only the tornado that struck Edwardsville on 27th October 1913, has been widely chronicled. Surely the early months of 1947 deserve equal importance. Whereas the tornado affected few people in the lower part of the Borough, the '1947 Winter' was suffered by all regions of Great Britain and in particular, Merthyr Tydfil.

The Editor of the Merthyr Express predicted that many people would be able to say in future years, "Ah! that was a winter in 1947. I know for I was snowed-up in a train."

Those, who lived through those difficult days, have vivid personal memories that have not dimmed during the intervening years. The events were frozen into recollections that will never thaw.

1947 set a standard to measure all future winters.

*   *   *

Forecasters had given no inkling of what was to happen between late January and the middle of March 1947. Yet those seven or eight weeks provided an ordeal unequalled in systematic meteorological records. With the exception of two brief, cold spells in the middle of December 1946 and early January 1947, the winter had been remarkably mild. With depressions moving in from the Atlantic, November and the early part of December 1946 had been very wet, warm and muggy. The middle of January 1947, too, was unusually warm but the 18th was to be the last mild day.

It had started to snow in the South East of England on 23rd January but the weather forecasters prophesied that it wouldn't last. However, it spread west and north accompanied by intense cold. By the 26th January 1947, snow covered the entire face of Britain. Even the south west was affected and seven inches of snow lay at both Scilly and the Lizard on 30th January. The South Wales Echo stated, "We are in the grip of one of the worst freeze ups since records were first kept in 1878."

At Ponsticill eighteen degrees of frost was recorded on 29th January 1947 but the following night Cardiff was even colder. There were intermittent snow showers during the week but the two inches that fell on the 29th stopped the Merthyr to Brecon and the Merthyr to Tredegar bus services. The railway services to and from Merthyr were not affected. Compared with other parts of the country, Merthyr had been fortunate in that there were no electricity cuts. However the Dowlais Hosiery Mills were closed for a few days owning to a fuel shortage and Welsh Cup Match between Merthyr and Cardiff had to be postponed.

*   *   *

A bitterly cold, penetrating, easterly wind blew for a solid month until 23rd February 1947. The temperature did not climb above Freezing Point any day from 11th to 23rd February 1947. Snow fell on some part of the country every day between 23rd January and 17th March 1947. There was an unrelieved dullness and no glimpse of the sun was recorded at Kew between the 2nd and 22nd February 1947. On 20th February the South Wales Echo showed a picture of the sun shining over Cardiff entitled—"The Stranger". Not liking what it saw, it had quickly disappeared from a land that had known nothing but frost, snow and a biting wind for nearly a month.

The United Kingdom experienced continuous snow cover until 13th March 1947. On 10th February there were drifts six feet deep in Cardiff Docks and the roads in Merthyr Tydfil were blocked. Council workmen were doing a fine job clearing the snow but shopkeepers and householders were urged to clear the pavements outside their shops and homes. It was a child's dream come true and there were pictures of an igloo in West Grove and a sleigh run in Dane Street. It was the eighteenth day for snow to fall in the Western Valley of Monmouthsire and the sixth day for its twenty thousand inhabitants to be without gas for lighting, heating and cooking owing to the freeze up of the coke ovens at Blaenavon. The sombreness of Post War Britain deepened as the weather did its worst. Even bread was rationed and coal shortages frequently caused power cuts. Food was a serious problem in many areas and hundreds used sleds and travelled miles to collect provisions from neighbouring towns. There was an Official Fuel Crisis for three weeks between 10th February and 3rd March. Power cuts extended to South Wales and the Government ordered the Merthyr Electrical Traction to reduce voltage by five per cent and imposed a ban between nine and twelve and two and four. The ban applied to schools, shops, offices, cinemas and household users but industry was exempted. Above Dowlais there was a drift twenty two feet deep and half a mile long and Ogilvie Colliery was virtually cut off. The Merthyr Express blamed the Minister of Fuel & Power for the Crisis and for not heeding warnings. A great coal getting drive was launched and miners in the South Wales Coalfield were urged to work on Sunday. The response was excellent with 581 men reporting to Merthyr Vale and 771 to Deep Navigation.

The South Wales Echo warned of heatless, lightless days ahead and the warning proved correct. Although there was a slight thaw on 10th February 1947, with a gradual easing of conditions, the following day temperatures fell below zero again and on the 24th they plunged to the Lows experienced at the end of January. Another blizzard in the middle of the month caused drifts as high as the bedroom windows in Galon Uchaf and an LMS engine on the Abergavenny line was buried for several days near Penywern before it was exhumed by a large gang of railwaymen.

People weren't the only sufferers. There was a lack of grazing on the mountains and the starving sheep and ponies raided the allotments, parks and cemeteries throughout the Borough. The Parks Superintendent reported that sheep had eaten a portion of the hayrick in Cefn Cemetery and shrubs had been grazed to the stumps. At Galon Uchaf ponies were following people carrying baskets. Councillors were at their wits end and they made numerous complaints against the local farmers. Probably more animals died from thirst than from hunger. The farmers would break the ice on the mountain streams but it refroze before the animals could drink. Before the end of February everyone had had enough especially the railwaymen who were working day and night to keep the traffic moving. No wonder they welcomed the arrival of an RAF crew planning to clear the lines at Dowlais Top and Cwmbargoed. Two jet engines, of the type fitted to the Gloster Meteor record-breaking aircraft, were mounted on a special railway wagon. When Flight Lieutenant Walton started the engines the noise was terrific but it was hoped that the exhausts would partly melt and partly blow away the snow. There were observers from the National Gas Turbine Experimental Establishment at Leicester; from the Rolls Royce Works and from the Great Western Railway. Unfortunately the experiments were not entirely successful so it was back to the picks and shovels.

The Meteorological Office estimated that with the exception of February 1895, it had been the coldest month recorded in England and Wales since 1881.

*   *   *

On Saturday, 1st March 1947, things were looking brighter. An Air Ministry expert said the snow was dying out and two days later a general thaw was reported to be on the way. At last after five weeks of Arctic weather, the end seemed to be in sight.

However, hopes were dashed when Tuesday the 4th and Wednesday the 5th March 1947 heralded the worst blizzard in living memory. There were twenty foot snow drifts with road and rail traffic paralysed. Merthyr people awoke to find the streets covered to a depth of more than a foot and there were tremendous drifts on the higher parts of the Borough.

On Tuesday, the 4th March, the 3pm train carrying between thirty and forty passengers from Newport to Brecon became stuck in a ten foot drift in the Pantywaun Cutting between Fochriw and Dowlais Top. Three light engines and a snow plough were sent to release the train but they, too, got snowed up. Railway officials managed to get sandwiches to the passengers but they had to spend the night in the train. The following morning the passengers dug their way out and were put up by the people of the isolated village of Fochriw.

Many people, including some miners who had worked the night shift in the Glynneath collieries, were marooned on Abernant Station from 3pm on Tuesday until 10am the next morning.

The 4.10pm train from Merthyr on Tuesday reached Brecon but on the return journey it ran into a deep drift on the Brecon side of the Torpantau Tunnel, 1200 ft above sea level. The driver, fireman, guard and about two dozen passengers had to spend the night in the train. The next morning a light engine was able to reach them with food and blankets. One hundred and fifty soldiers and fifty others worked throughout Wednesday to release the train but forty hours had elapsed before the passengers, many in a weak state, were rescued.

Between forty and sixty vehicles were marooned on Rhymney Common on Tuesday night but the occupants managed to complete their journeys on foot. A large number of people from Tredegar, Ebbw Vale and the Rhymney Valley were stranded in Merthyr on Tuesday night and the police had a busy time fixing accommodation for them in local hotels and public houses.

Shops, offices and factories were short staffed on Wednesday and Thursday because there were no conveyances to bring them to Town from the outlying areas. Hundreds of people braved the blizzard to collect milk from Conways and bread from the local bakeries.

On Wednesday night, a police message was broadcast on the Merthyr Rediffusion Service stating that one hundred workers from the Borough employed at Thorn's Electrical Industries factory at Rhigos, were stranded on Hirwaun Station,. It added that the manager was arranging accommodation for the night.

Later there was a radio appeal for all able-bodied men to help to clear the roads and rails. The effect on coal output was serious because thousands of miners in South Wales and hundreds from the Merthyr Valley were unable to get to work. Many volunteered to help clear the lines to the mines. So did many unemployed men, glad to leave the Dole queue and earn some money simply shovelling. Although the sun was shining brightly on Thursday, rail and road traffic in Merthyr was chaotic. At 7am on Thursday a train left Merthyr for Cardiff but it ran into a drift near Troedythiw and the passengers had to walk back to Town.

In Pant, council officials climbed twelve foot drifts to collect the rents from bedroom windows.

Thousands of sheep on the mountain sides were buried beneath the snow and it was reported that starving foxes burrowed twenty feet on the Brecon Beacons to reach the animals.

The Jet engines were recalled and this time they successfully cleared the Ponsticill to Pant line using twelve gallons of fuel per minute. Yet on

Friday, 7th March, road and rail arteries were cut off for the third successive day.

Meanwhile at the opencast coal site, five hundred feet above Brynmawr, twenty eight degrees of frost had been recorded and the fierce wind caused the formation of horizontal icicles. A freak storm had brought down the telephone and electricity wires and the seven thousand inhabitants of the highest town in South Wales were isolated for days. Helicopters dropped supplies of yeast on Brynmawr Rugby ground so that local bakers could continue to make bread. Despite the appaling conditions, the one hundred and fifty men worked a seven day week on the coal site or helping to clear the streets of Brynmawr. As food and fuel supplies ran low, two vans of meat, snowbound in Beaufort, were stripped of their contents and three engines, marooned at Nantyglo, were emptied of coal.

By 10th March, a general thaw was spreading throughout South Wales and the worst winter the local people had ever known drew to a close.

Then came the rain!

The Meteorological Office's Report for March 1947 stated—"The thawing of the snow accompanies by frequent rain in the second half of the month caused unprecedented floods over large areas of England and Wales. It was the wettest March in the long record going back to 1869."

The Editor of the Merthyr Express had been scathing in his criticism of the Ministry of Fuel & Power; the Air Ministry forecasters and others. However, after a visit to London, he expressed his heartfelt sympathy for the people of Reading and Maidenhead in the Thames Valley.

Mountain streams were turned into raging torrents and the swollen rivers carried the carcases of dead animals to the sea.

Merthyr Tydfil's altitude had been a handicap; now it was an asset.

*   *   *

Undoubtedly memories of 1947 will raise many questions.

Did the experiences of the War Years help people to cope with the ordeal of 1947? One old miner said—"It was a white blitz and maybe it was last time the Valleys were real old type communities. Everyone pulled together."

Did rationing and fair shares prevent bitterness and create a community spirit? With the threat of Global Warming will there ever be a repeat of 1947?

*   *   *

An Australian Visitor—
Sir Samuel Griffith in South Wales, 1887

by FRED HOLLEY & V. A. HOLLEY

A sequence of events,which commenced in 1885, resulted in Sir Samuel Griffith, Queen's Counsel, Knight Commander of St. Michael and St. George, Premier of Queensland, coming to South Wales in 1887, to visit his birthplace, Merthyr Tydfil.

Sir Samuel visited London in 1887, the year of Queen Victoria's Golden Jubilee, to attend a Conference corresponding to the present day Commonwealth Prime Ministers' Conference, and took this opportunity to visit his birthplace.

This essay is an account of Sir Samuel's visit to South Wales, gleaned from newspaper sources, including the Merthyr Express, South Wales Daily News,and the Western Mail.

We are indebted to Morien of the Western Mail for some background to Sir Samuel's visit to South Wales,and details of his departure from Queensland:–

"In November 1886 I called attention to the very interesting fact that the present Prime Minister of the great Colony of Queensland is a native of Merthyr Tydfil, a town which,it can be safely stated, has sent forth to the world more men who have become distinguished than any other in the Principality.

At an annual meeting of the Congregational Union of England and Wales, held in 1885 at the City Temple, London,over which the late Rev. Thomas Rees, D. D., Swansea, would have presided had he not died before the meeting took place, I saw a venerable preacher ascending the platform, in compliance with the request of the President (the Rev. Dr. John Thomas, Liverpool). The name of the venerable gentleman was the Rev. E. Griffith, and no sooner did he begin to address the distinguished gathering than he

83

referred to Wales, and to the lamented Thomas Rees as his old friend. This was followed by his relating old recollections of Merthyr Tydfil, where, he stated, he himself began to preach many years before. It was from Merthyr Tydfil, the patriarch said, he had emigrated to Australia. And out of the fullness of his heart,and as if feeling he was "home" once more among relatives and friends,the proud Welsh father told the "family circle" that his "boy" was the Prime Minister of Queenland, Sir S. W .Griffith.

A copy of the Western Mail containing the article in question reached Sir Samuel, as described in the following letter which has just reached me from the Colony:– Clydach Cottage, Bridge-Street, Fortitude Valley, Brisbane. January 20th 1887. My dear "Morien",

On the 10.1.1887 I received from home (Dolycoed, Llanwrtyd) a copy of the Western Mail containing an article by you on our distinguished Premier, the Right Hon. Sir S. W. Griffith. On the 11th I forwarded the paper to Sir Samuel, and on the next day I received an autograph letter from him of which the following is a copy:– Colonial Secretary's Office, Brisbane. 11.1.1887.

Dear Sir, Accept my thanks for the copy of the Western Mail of the 22.11.1886, and for your kind and complimentary letter forwarding it. I confess that it gives me great pleasure to think that I am not unknown in my native land, which I hope to have time to re-visit when I am in England, in a few weeks time.

Yours very truly, S.W.Griffith.

The letter of my correspondent then proceeds:–

'On Tuesday evening a farewell banquet was given to Sir Samuel, and I send you cuttings of yesterday's newspaper containing a full report of the proceedings. Besides being undoubtedly the most popular man in Brisbane, the most brilliant politician in Queensland, and the most able statesman in the whole of Australia, Sir Samuel is a true friend to his Cambrian fellow countrymen, and honours their institutions. During the second week of last November, at considerable inconvenience to himself, he presided at an Eisteddfod held by the Welsh at Gympie; that is an awkward place to get at, and he had to travel 100 miles by steamer to Maryborough and thence by rail. If you wish you may publish this letter and thus let my friends know that I am alive.They will be glad to learn that I have attained my object in coming to Queensland viz, the restoration of my dear wife to health.

Os bydd yr ychydig linellau hyn yn dderbyniol, mi a ysgrifenaf etto.

Yours, etc. Ben Jones.

The cuttings referred to prove that the banquet was a very grand affair and that it was attended by the leading men of the Colony. It is interesting to find that the grace was offered up by the Rev. E. Griffith, the Prime Minister's father.

Before Sir Samuel got up to speak, the orchestra struck up "The March of the Men of Harlech", in reference to the Premier's Cambrian origin. The report of his speech occupied three columns and a half of the newspaper. It is most interesting to note some soul-stirring verses in reference to Britain, which were sung on the occasion. Here they are:–

Hurrah! for Old England, hurrah!
Dear Homeland,we greet thee afar;
What matter if ocean its billows roll high?
What matter if wide leagues of earth 'tween us lie?
Old England is ours, tis the boast that we make.
Aye ready to do or to die for her sake.
Chorus.
For shoulder to shoulder we'll stand,boys,
True for aye to the old Motherland,boys,
　　Her sons we are ever
　　No foe e'er can sever
Our hearts from the old Motherland, boys!, etc.

I believe Sir Samuel has reached London. He will probably be in Wales shortly. Will the Metropolis of Wales give him a welcome? Will Merthyr, his native town, the old town of Iron Kings, accord him a welcome worthy of him and of itself? He is a worthy son of the Sparta of Western Europe—Cymru!—and deserves all the honour Cymru can confer upon him. "Harlech,cyfod dy faneri!"

Arrival and Reception at Cardiff, Pontypridd and Merthyr Tydfil
The due arrival in South Wales on Wednesday of the Hon. Sir Samuel Griffith, Q.C., K.C.M.G., a Merthyr-born man, who now occupies the proud position of Premier of the rising colony of Queensland, was naturally an event full of incident and interest. There had not been much time for preparation on the part of those who wished to prove their good wishes but the reception accorded him was, nevertheless, of a most enthusiastic kind. Sir Samuel arrived in Cardiff by the 3.13pm train from London. He was met at the

G.W.R. station by The Mayor of Cardiff, The Archdeacon of Llandaff, Mr.W. L. Daniel, High Constable of Merthyr, Mr. F. S. Johnstone, and a few other gentlemen.

After some little delay, Sir S. Griffith drove to the Taff Vale Station, whence he departed for Merthyr,where he will be the guest of Mr. W. T. Crawshay at Cyfarthfa Castle. Lady Griffith would have accompanied her husband to Wales were it not that her physicians absolutely prohibited the journey, she remained in London, ill with pneumonia

When the Taff Vale train which contained the visitor arrived at Pontypridd, there was an enthusiastic demonstration during the stoppage. Mr. W. Abraham, M.P., (Mabon), induced the Premier to say a few words to the assembled people. Sir Samuel was exceedingly sorry he was unable to address them in their native language. He said he would address them in his next best, English. He observed there was in the Colony which he represented plenty of room for all of them,ample work and good pay. He thanked them from his heart for the kindly welcome they had given him.

At the Merthyr Railway Station everybody was on the quivive for the approach of the train. It arrived with characteristic punctuality at about five o'clock. As it neared the station there was a continuous discharge of detonators. The platform was occupied by MASSED CHOIRS assembled (under the leadership of Mr. Tom Brice), the BAND of the Merthyr detachment 2nd G.V.R. (led by Mr. Jones), and a number of general spectators, a front space being preserved by Inspector Rodman and other members of the police force. The members of the reception committee present were Messrs. J. Jones, David E. Jones, J. Vaughan, secretary, Dr. Biddle and John Jenkins.

When the band stopped the choir,of six hundred voices,sang the first verse of an ode, which was composed for the occasion by W. R. Price, (Gwyddonfryn), to the music of the Harlech march,a spirited accompaniment being played by the band, and the public outside the station raising loud cheers. While the first verse was being sung, Sir Samuel walked down the platform to a central point with his host,Mr. W. T. Crawshay, and was afterwards introduced to Mr. Smyth, J.P., Mr. T. White,and other local gentlemen. He was also handed a framed copy of the words which had been sung. These commenced with the injunction:–

Merthyr Tydfil, cwyd yr awrhon
I ddadblygu iaith dy galon
Wrth roesawu un o'th feibion
Godwyd i fawrhad.

In the second verse Sir Samuel was described as follows "Cymro yw; mae'n caru Cymru: Yn mhlith mawrion ni wna i gwadu."

The Premier seemed to be delighted with his reception, and took off his hat and bowed courteously, with a genial smile upon his face, in acknowledgement of the cheering which arose on all sides when there ensued a pause in the singing.

The band and the choristers then marched out of the station, and Sir Samuel shortly afterwards followed, and took his seat with Mr. Crawshay in the latter gentleman's carriage, which was open.

A procession was formed, Mr. Superintendent Thomas, the marshal, was at the head on horseback, and a body of police officers led the way, followed by many of the vocalists, and others, after whom came the band, the committee-men, and other townsmen including Mr. T. Bowen Jones, Mr. Morgan, Mr. Sibbering and the Rev. Rees Evans.

The carriage, drawn by a pair of fine horses, came next, and carriages at the rear contained Mr. Tudor Crawshay and Judge Gwilym Williams, also a guest at Cyfarthfa.

The High-street was lined with school children, the flags and banners carried by the little ones lending quite a gay appearance to the old and some-what circuitous thoroughfare. There was a temporary stoppage near the High Constable's residence, the occasion of which was the presentation to the Premier at his carriage door by a young lady, Miss Florence Daniel, of a choice bouquet, which she offered in the name of the Market-square School.

The windows of the houses along the line of route were crowded with spectators, and at some of the premises there was a festive display of bunting. Sir Samuel must have been struck by the neat appearance of the Sunday scholars, not forgetting those of the Protestant Sunday-school, who wore, for the first time, bright Jubilee medals, which had been distributed by Dr. Biddle and the other managers. The procession passed up the Brecon Road, and at Grawen the committee divided. The visitor passed through (the toll gates) and continued his musical drive to the gates of Cyfarthfa Castle, the High Con-stable and others returning to town on foot.

Visit to Cwmtaff

On Thursday in the forenoon, Sir Samuel, accompanied by his host, Mr. W. T. Crawshay, drove through several parts of the town and district. He was subsequently driven to Cwmtaff by Mr.Crawshay, Mr. W. L. Daniel and other gentlemen were included in the party. The visitor thus had the opportunity of inspecting the extensive water works in course of construction by the Cardiff Corporation.

The Merthyr Banquet

On Thursday evening the Prime Minister was entertained at a banquet given by the leading inhabitants of the town at the Bush Hotel. The spacious assembly room had during the day undergone a complete transformation, and by the aid of mirrors, curtains, bunting and choice plants and flowers fixed on brackets, it presented, under the gaslight, a peculiarly attractive appearance. The plants and flowers were arranged by Mr. E. H. Brattram, florist, Pontmorlais, who deserves the greatest credit for the taste he displayed therein. A beautiful banner of red silk on which was inscribed "Welcome Sir Samuel Griffith" hung just above a large mirror placed at the back of the cross-table which stood upon a carpeted dais. The tables were laid with a sumptuousness that spoke volumes for the resources and catering capabilities of the worthy host, Mr. Michael.

Shortly after seven o'clock Sir Samuel and the distinguished party from Cyfarthfa Castle entered the room,and the company remained standing until they had reached their seats at the cross-table. Grace before-and after meat was said by the Rector of Merthyr, the Rev. D. Lewis. The High Constable presided, supported at the cross-table on the right by Sir Samuel, the guest of the evening, Mrs. W. L. Daniel, Mr. W. T. Crawshay, the Hon. Mrs. Ruthven and Mrs. Tudor Crawshay, and on the left by Mrs. W. T. Crawshay, Judge Gwilym Williams, Mrs. Rose Mary Crawshay and Mr. Tudor Crawshay, High Sheriff of Glamorganshire.

Among the other ladies and gentlemen present were Mr. and Mrs. David Williams, Henstaff Court, Mr. Frank James and the Misses James, Mr. and Mrs. T. H. Bailey, Mr. and Mrs. Peter Williams, Mr. T. W. Lewis and Miss Lewis, Tydfil House, Dr. and Mrs. Biddle, Mr. and Mrs. Davis, Morriston, Mr. and Mrs. Thomas Edwards, Cefn, Mrs. Bishop, Mrs. J. D. W.illiams, The Rector of Merthyr, Rev. D. Lewis, Rev. J. G. James, pastor, Market Square Congregational Church, Major Jones, the American Consul at Cardiff, Lt-Col David Rees Lewis, William Lewis, Penydarren (House), Messrs. W. Smyth, J.P., T. Williams, J.P., D.Davies, High Constable of Aberdare, W. J. Jones, John Vaughan, solicitor, G. C. James, John Gabe, J. Thomas, Deputy Chief Constable of Police for Glamorganshire, Thomas Thomas, Ironmonger, D. Phillips, Draper, L. P. Jones, M.F.H., J. O. White, R. Harrap, J. G. Rogers, Cyfarthfa, H. Southey, Christmas Evans, D. Abraham, C. Wilkins, historian,

W. Beddoe, T. Jenkins, Pant, J. Sibbering, Owen Morgan, MORIEN, journalist and local historian, F. Sonley Johnstone, Cardiff, J. Thomas, Western Mail, John G. E. Astle, South Wales Daily News, F. J. Harries, Merthyr Express. Mr. David Williams occupied the Vice-Chair.

During the "masticatory" proceedings Mr. Lewis's talented orchestral string band played an excellent selection of music. The energy displayed by Mr. John Vaughan as secretary of the committee should not go unmentioned. Mr. Vaughan worked hard and zealously, but,unfortunately, was not able to participate to the full in the enjoyment of Thursday, in consequence of an indisposition from which he suffered during that day.

The After-Dinner Speeches

The following toasts were honoured:–
1. "The Queen" was proposed by the Chairman, also 2. "The Prince and Princess of Wales". 3. "The Bishop and Clergy of all Denominations" was proposed by Judge Gwilym Williams and responded to by the Rector of Merthyr, the Rev. D. Lewis. The Rev. J. G. James, Market Square Congregational Church, also responded. 4. "The Army, Navy and Auxiliary Forces" was proposed by Mr. W. T. Crawshay and responded to by Lt. Col. D. Rees Lewis. Sir Samuel Griffith" was proposed by the Chairman, W. L. Daniel, High Constable, and responded to by Sir Samuel. 6. "The Imperial Parliament" was submitted by Major Jones, Cardiff, American Consul, Mr. G. C. James responded. 7. "Mr. Tudor Crawshay" was proposed by Mr. F. Sonley Johnstone. 8. "The Town and Trade of Merthyr" was proposed by Mr. D. Davis, Morriston, and responded to by Mr. Peter Williams and Mr. David Williams. 9. "The Ladies" was submitted by Mr. David Williams and responded to by Mrs. Rose Mary Crawshay.

Sir Samuel's Health Proposed

The Chairman proposed the health of Sir Samuel Griffith, their distinguished visitor and honoured guest.He ventured to think that this toast would receive ample justice at the hands of those present. (Applause). Unfortunately, perhaps, the honoured name of the guest of the evening was a few weeks ago comparatively unknown to them, but no time had been lost, when it became known that he intended visiting the place of his birth, to prepare a welcome for him as cordial and as enthusiastic as it would be possible to give so distinguished a visitor. He (the Chairman) was looking through the records of Queensland and its legislation only a few days ago, when a remark made by one of his children struck him. "Why papa" was the exclamation referred to,' Mr. Griffith appears to have done everything". If they looked at the records he had mentioned they would find that some of the most beneficial measures which had been passed in connection with that Colony had been introduced through the indefatigable efforts of their distinguished guest.

Let them take their memory back for a moment to the time when their honoured visitor was borne a baby from the town of his nativity. Little did the father, who had so endeared himself to the congregation at Market square, think as he took the mother and baby away from the old town that it would be his proud privilege to revisit the old country as a delegate from Queensland, and tell his old friends that his "boy" was at that moment Prime Minister of the Colony of Queensland. They had not the honoured father present that evening, but they had the distinguished son, and he felt assured that no stranger had ever entered the town of Merthyr who had been greeted with so much enthusiasm or had become so popular as Sir Samuel Griffith. The assembly that evening was, as Judge Williams had remarked, a representative assembly. They had representatives there from all parts of the district, and embracing all shades of public opinion; they had the learned professions, they had trade represented, and they had the great iron kings of the district represented. (Applause). He ventured to say that the action of their esteemed friend Mr. Crawshay and his lady, in so readily offering the hospitalities of Cyfarthfa Castle to their distinguished guest, had done much to endear them to the people of Merthyr. (Applause). They were extremely sorry that Lady Griffith, in consequence of an attack of pneumonia, was unable to be in attendance that evening, to witness the enthusiasm manifested in the reception of her husband. Her Ladship, if she had been present, would, he was sure, have felt prouder than ever of her husband. The committee, in anticipation of the presence of Lady Griffith, had arranged to present her with a bouquet of flowers, the purity of which would represent the purity of the desire of the people of Merthyr to recognise greatness. This bouquet Sir Samuel would be asked to receive on behalf of Lady Griffith. (Applause). In concluding, the Chairman remarked that in re-visiting his birthplace the sentiment of the poet must have appealed strongly to the feelings of their distinguished guest:–

"Breathes there a man with soul so dead
Who never to himself has said
This is my own,my native land?"

The Merthyr Presentation

Mr. W. J. Jones presented Sir Samuel with a beautifully-illuminated Address in album form. It was engrossed by the celebrated Messrs. Waterlow, and on the cover contained this inscription in gold letters:– "To the Honourable Sir Samuel Walker Griffiths, K.C.M.G., 1887." The text ran as follows:– To The Hon. Sir Samuel Walker Griffith, Q.C., K.C.M.G. Respected Sir, It is with unfeigned pleasure that we welcome you amongst us, only too proud to know that you are one of the many sons of eminence whom the old town of Merthyr has produced, and who, from no adventitious chances of fortune, but from their own energy and talent, have gained high and merited distinction in the world. We feel that to you especially this high meed of praise is unquestionably due, for at an age when most young men are undecided as to their course in life you had won the highest scholarship in the colony, and were in the track for distinctive position, and in your young manhood were Attorney-General and Minister of Public Instruction. May we, without undue eulogy, add even more than this, though the highest honours of the profession were then within your grasp, you were never allured by them, but firmly refused all temptations in order to devote yourself to the work of the Government of which you are now the head? As we recall your achievements we are reminded of other sons of ours who have filled high judicial positions in the Metropolis of the British Empire and in India, Lord Justice James and Lord Chief Justice Morgan, of India; of Petherick, associated with the discovery of the Nile; of Penry Williams, a painter of rank; of Joseph Edwards, a sculptor of great merit. We have the satisfaction of knowing, too, that the first mayor of Middleborough, Mr. Edward Williams, was a Merthyr man, and that the leading authority in mining engineering upon whom the distinction of Knighthood was lately conferred, Sir W. T. Lewis, claims Merthyr as his birthplace. To these we might add many others who have in one way or the other gained celebrity, and whose names are remembered by us, some with affection, and all with honour. But sir, as we do so, we can but repeat that to these men, as to you, we have been unable to accord any other than our hearty sentiments of respect and congratulation. While you and other noble Merthyrians have risen in the world, the old town has fallen away from its position of being the largest populated town of Wales, and the most enterprising and hopeful, while places which were small in comparison have received all the advantages due to our minerals and our manufactures. To have kept pace with our sons' achievements we should have had our Charter of Incorporation at the least,and the unpretending banquet we welcome you to should be in a Town Hall, and presided over by a Mayor.

Still, if Merthyr has not kept pace, it has made itself famous in every land from the excellence of its coal, iron and steel, and when to this we link the attainments of our own distinguished children, we can have no cause for regret in the part Merthyr has played, and no reason to doubt that it has graven its name deeply upon the history of the country. Not to Merthyr, then, the obscure and unknown, do we welcome you, and again we heartily congratulate you and pray that time may deal kindly with you, adding many years of life and health and happiness to your portion and still higher distinctions to those you have so brilliantly won.

Signed W. L. Daniel, High Constable, Chairman. John Vaughan, Secretary. Dated this 14th. day of April, 1887.

Owen Morgan, MORIEN, then, by request, delivered a brief address, in which he spoke of the pride he felt in having been the first to introduce Sir Samuel's name to his native country.

The Band then played "Hen Wlad fy Nhadau", the company singing the words.

Sir Samuel's Speech at Merthyr Tydfil

Sir Samuel, upon rising to respond, was greeted with rounds upon rounds of applause. He said he felt quite unable properly to express his feelings to show his gratitude at the reception accorded to him upon coming to "Hen wlad fy nhadau". He paid a high compliment to the choir who sang the ode at the railway station on Wednesday upon his arrival by train, he said that everything had been done to make his visit to Merthyr a thing to be remembered. The only thing that marred his pleasure was the absence of Lady Griffith. Her Ladyship had looked forward with the greatest pleasure to being with him, but her medical adviser had peremptorily forbidden her to leave London. He was sure she would be delighted to hear of the kindness he had received at their hands. Proceeding, Sir Samuel said that he had for a long time taken an interest in all matters connected with the Principality in Queensland, and some six months ago he presided at an Eisteddfod held in one of the towns in the goldfields. Speaking upon the subject of Imperial Federation, he said there was a great lack of knowledge in the old country of the different parts of the Empire, and he thought it would be a good thing if they knew a little more about one another. It would be to the advantage of the Empire if more information respecting the Colonies were given in the London press. There was a largely increasing tendency on the part of the Government and the leading statesmen of England to take the Colonies into council, and the

Conference which he had come to attend was the best proof of that. He thought it would be found, when they had concluded the sittings, that very important steps had been taken towards cementing the union of the Empire in Australia. Sir Samuel pointed out that they had extensive free institutions; they managed their affairs exactly as they pleased, subject, of course, to the paramount authority of her Majesty's Ministers, who, however, never interfered. They had the advantage there of starting with a clean sheet; they were not trammelled by any old prejudices, or very few; they were not conservative in their ways by any means; and they were never afraid of anything because it was new. At the same time, they had the light of history to guide them. In that they found a good many lessons to profit by, and also a good many pitfalls to avoid. In Australia it would never occur to anyone to have an Established Church; and as for the ballot, they had had that ever so long. In many other particulars they had tried experiments which had been successful. For instance, they had a law relating to land, similar to that proposed in the Bill recently introduce by the Lord Chancellor, in force for twenty five years in all the Colonies. Now, education was admitted to be a matter of State concern, and in Queensland it was free. It was secular, but every facility was given for imparting religious instruction.

He ventured to think that the original trouble in Ireland had arisen from the unfortunate land laws, by which large estates came into few hands. In the newer countries they had an enormous tract of valuable land belonging to the State, and the Government had laid it down as a principle and had induced Parliament to accept it, that they would not part with the freehold of that land except to people who intended to occupy it. Then throughout Queensland they had a system of local government. (Applause). They had no Mayor and Corporation in Merthyr. In Queensland if the inhabitants of the place did not elect officers the Government itself would appoint them. (Laughter). The roads were maintained by the local authorities, the Government contributing a certain proportion of the necessary expenses. That was a system which he thought might well be adopted in England and other parts of the world. (Applause). There was this to be said about a system of local government. It taught people to take an interest in the management of their own affairs. In Queensland they had ample room for people from all parts of the Empire. There was a surplus population in this country, and he hoped it would go to the British dominions and not elsewhere, so that they might build up a united Empire. (Applause). Referring to the voluntary help afforded to England by Australia during the late Egyptian war, Sir Samuel remarked that the

Colonists recognised that they belonged to the old country, and that it was their duty to share her dangers as well as benefit by her protection. (Applause). They did not want the mother country to bear the expense of defending her children; they were quite ready and prepared to take their share in the work. (Cheers). He hoped the result of the proceedings this year in England would be to give them a better opinion and a better idea of each other. For his own part he hoped to be able to do some good work. He had been told that evening that he had already performed some good work for his Colony. (Applause). As he had now occupied the position of Prime Minister for considerably over three years he fancied this must be so, and he hoped when he returned to be able to still do more in his country's service. He was not old; his health was good, and he looked forward to a many years' continuance of good health and vigour. He did not believe he looked very old, although he was the veteran of his Colony in experience. (Cheers). It had always pleased him to think that he was the youngest member of his own Government. He knew he should never forget Merthyr Tydfil. (Loud cheers). He could never forget the kindness he had received at the hands of its inhabitants or the cordial welcome that had been extended to him. He ventured to hope that in the future people in the Principality would take a somewhat greater interest in the affairs of his part of the world than they had done hitherto. He again thanked them most deeply for the welcome accorded him, and he asked them to believe that he would endeavour in the future to bring no disgrace on the name of Merthyr. (Cheers).

Further Toasts Proposed

The toast of the "Imperial Parliament" was submitted by Major Jones, of Cardiff. The genial American Consul said that the coming from Cardiff there to witness the ceremonials of that day had given him sincere gratification. Merthyr had turned out a great many men who had attained distinction in the world. Let them search in the fields of literature or the ranks of industry, and they would find the Merthyr boy benefiting humanity, and bringing credit and distinction to himself and the town in which he was born. Having paid a tribute to the Queen and Parliament, Major Jones proceeded to deal with the question of Imperial Federation. The links of the Empire welded together, and the Colonies represented in St. Stephens, would be, he said, a realisation of Government, which the dreams of Caesar never contemplated. This was not an idea which recommended itself to all, but it was an idea which, if not consummated by the statesmen of today, must, at all events, be dealt with by the statesmen of the future. It would be a glorious day for this country when that realisation was brought about. (Applause). The Band played "The Imperial Parliament".

Mr. G. C. James, in responding, said it was impossible to forecast what the ultimate material benefit of Imperial Federation would be; but whatever the result of the deliberations in which Sir Samuel Griffith had taken so distinguished and prominent a part, one could not but rejoice at the feelings which had prompted the representatives of the Colonists to come over to this Conference. (Applause). He had no doubt, whatever measures would be referred and brought to pass, that the names of the gentlemen who were now taking part in this important business would in the years to come be handed down to posterity and be revered by future generations, and among them the name of Sir Samuel Griffith. (Cheers).

Mr. F. Sonley Johnstone, at the invitation of the High Constable, proposed the health of Mr. Tudor Crawshay, who had just been appointed High Sheriff of Glamorganshire. The name of Crawshay appeared to him to be about as old as the name of Merthyr. (Hear, hear). They were almost synonyms, for it would be very difficult to speak about Merthyr without introducing the name of Crawshay. When Merthyr was mentioned that name must be known, and he was pleased to have the opportunity, unexpected to him, of asking them to drink to the health of the High Sheriff of Glamorganshire. Referring to the depression in trade, he hoped there was a new era of prosperity in store for the town. (Hear, hear).

Mr. Tudor Crawshay replied, and spoke of the lively interest he had always felt in the progress of Merthyr.

Mr. D. Davis, Morriston, the senior parishioner of Merthyr, proposed the toast of the "Town and Trade of Merthyr". Mr. Davis remarked that the tin-plate trade was now the industry of the country, and he was sorry that he was, some time ago, unable to obtain sufficient support in Merthyr to establish his tin works there. He expressed a hope that Queensland would become a customer of this neighbourhood, and referred to the pleasure it would give him to see a good rail works established at Penydarren and a large tin works at Plymouth. (Applause).

Turning to Mrs. Rose Mary Crawshay, he said he was glad to see her present, and looking so well. (Applause). They were all proud of her, and her name was a household word in the neighbourhood.

The Band played "March of the men of Harlech".

Mr. Peter Williams and Mr. David Williams having responded in felicitous terms, the latter gentleman proposed the health of "The Ladies" to which Mrs. Rose Mary Crawshay made a graceful response.

The proceedings then terminated.

The Return To Cardiff

Sir Samuel Griffith returned to Cardiff from Merthyr Tydfil at ten minutes to twelve on Friday morning. The distinguished visitor, who was the guest of the Mayor, Mr. Morgan Morgan, was met at the Taff Vale Railway Station by his Worship and the Town-clerk, Mr. J. L. Wheatley, and on alighting from the railway carriage was cordially welcomed. He at once entered the carriage of the Mayor, and was driven to his Worship's residence in Cathedral-road, where he partook of luncheon.

Subsequently Sir Samuel was shown through the Castle by the Mayor. In consequence of a prior engagement to attend a meeting in support of the Church House at the Town-hall, his Worship was unable to accompany Sir Samuel to the docks, a visit to which took place in the afternoon.

The Cardiff Presentation

At six o'clock the members of the Town Council and a large number of the guests invited to the banquet given by the Mayor in honour of the visit to Cardiff of Sir Samuel W. Griffith, Premier of Queensland, met in the Council Chamber for the purpose of receiving the distinguished guest of the evening, and of presenting him with an Address of welcome. After a wait of a few minutes, the Mayor, to whose kindly thoughtfulness the initial steps were due, robed and preceded by the mace bearers, and accompanied by Sir Samuel, the Town-clerk, also robed, and the Mayors of Newport and Brecon, wearing their chains of office, entered the Chamber.

In a few words the Mayor called upon the Town-clerk to read the Address, beautifully illuminated and designed in the highest art by Messrs. Daniel Owen and Co., of Cardiff, and encased in morocco.

The text of the Address was as follows:–

BOROUGH OF CARDIFF.

To the Right Hon. Sir Samuel W. Griffith, K.C.M.G., Premier and Colonial Secretary of Queensland.

Sir, We the Mayor, Aldermen and Burgesses of the Borough of Cardiff desire, on behalf of the inhabitants, to offer you our hearty welcome to this ancient Borough, the Metropolis and chief port of the Principality of Wales, and also our sincere congratulations in your return to this your native County of Glamorgan, after an absence of many years. It is a matter of great pleasure to us that a native of this County has attained the high position of Premier of Queensland, a part of the largest and most important of one of the most loyal of our Colonies. We notice with extreme satisfaction your distinguished ability as a statesman and the many constitutional reforms you have advocated and passed, and congratulate ourselves on your having been at all times a true friend to this country and to those with whom you have come in contact in the land of your adoption, and that you have at all times honoured the ancient rights, customs and institutions of Wales. We confidently trust that you may be long spared to occupy the proud position now held by you over a free and enlightened people, to aid the development of their natural resources, and to witness their growing happiness and prosperity, and we fervently hope that your visit to Great Britain may tend to cement the friendly relations now existing between the two countries.

Dated this 15th. day of April. 1887. The common seal of the Mayor, Aldermen and Burgesses of the said Borough of Cardiff was hereunto affixed in the presence of Morgan Morgan. Mayor. J. L. Wheatley. Town-clerk.

The Cardiff Banquet

The company then moved to the Assembly-room along the corridor, which, for the nonce, had been transformed into a conservatory, beautiful with glorious foliage, while along the sides,as a guard of honour, were placed the members of the Police Band and the Fire Brigade.The tables had also been charmingly bedecked, the flowers being kindly sent from Cardiff Castle. During the progress of the banquet the Police Band, under the baton of Mr. Paul Draper, discoursed a choice selection of music.

Miss Annie T. Jones,on the harp,and the Llandaff Orpheus Glee Union also doing excellent musical service.

Mr. T. George, of Cathays, Cardiff, catered in his accustomed complete manner, while the wines, supplied by Messrs. Stevens, of Cardiff, could not have been bettered. As a compliment to the guest of the evening, several brands of colonial wine were placed on the table.

The following was the menu:– *Soup:* Mock Turtle, Jardiniere. *Fish:* Salmon and shrimp sauce, Turbot and lobster sauce, Fried Fillets of soles. *Entrees:* Sweetbread and truffles, Cutlets and mushrooms, Compote of pigeons. *Removes:* Quarters of lamb, Sirloins of beef, Roast and boiled turkeys, York hams, Chicken, Ox tongues, Saddles of mutton. *Game:* Prairie hens, Guinea fowls. *Entremets:* Jubilee and Newmarket puddings, Tourtes a la Princesse. *Trifles:* Curacoa, Noyeau and Dantzic jellies, Pine, Strawberry and Vanilla creams. *Compotes of Fruit. Ice Puddings. Cheese Omelettes, Deserts:* Pineapples, hothouse grapes, nuts, bananas, glace fruits, etc. *Coffee.*

The end of the menu was reached, then the Mayor gave the usual loyal toasts, which were warmly honoured.

Mr. R. E. Spencer gave the toast of "The Bishop and Clergy of the Diocese and Ministers of all Denominations" coupling with it the names of The Right Rev. the Lord Bishop of Llandaff, The Very Rev. Dean Vaughan, and The Rev. A. Tilly.

The Bishop of Llandaff in responding said the progress of the Church had become very rapid. He was opening churches at the rate of one a month. (Applause). He had opened one in February, one in March and one the day previous and another he had to open in May and he trusted that progress would be continued. With reference to his Nonconformist brethren, he hoped that the only rivalry would be who should be most devoted to their noble work.

Dean Vaughan, in response to calls, after speaking more particularly to the toast, went on to say that he could not but look upon that gathering as, in one sense, a union of the new world with the old. (Hear, hear). That new world, he knew, liked to come back sometimes and revive associations, which, if not personal, were at least hereditary. The old world had much to learn from the new. (Hear, hear). It was a privilege of the old to receive back the sons of the new with the honour which was their due. He thought a visit like this of an illustrious stranger to the home of his birth was a serious blow to the foolish slang—he could call it nothing else—which exclaimed! "Wales for the Welsh" (Applause). The field was the world, and he said "The World for the Welsh". (Loud applause). If Wales were for the Welsh, then they opened themselves to the retort "The Welsh for Wales" whereas he said "The World for the Welsh (applause)—and the Welsh for the World". (Renewed applause.)

They had served the world well, and he could not admit that a Welshman who came back to the home of his ancestry, who had been for generations serving Wales beyond the border, had any need to repair home in the white sheet of the prodigal or the penitent (hear, hear) or to say "Give me a little earth for charity" He (the speaker) claimed a little earth in Wales as the reward of a life spent in the service of Wales, in their common country, England and Wales, whom, concluded he, "God forbid should ever be sundered". (Loud applause).

A Toast To Sir Samuel

Archdeacon Griffiths on rising to propose the toast of Sir Samuel Griffith, was received with loud and prolonged cheers. What, he asked did that mighty gathering of the leading citizens of Cardiff, and of representatives from the surrounding neighbourhood, mean? There was no man more keenly alive to a sense of duty than the Mayor of Cardiff, and it was patriotism that welled into his heart, it was love of the fatherland, it was a feeling of pride that one of the sons of his own country who had obtained a position which reflected honour, not only upon himself, but upon the country to which he belonged, which prompted him to propose their present assemblage. (Applause). Hence also had that brilliant company gathered together.

Personally he might say he had never heard much of the sentiment deprecated by the Dean of Llandaff, namely "Wales for the Welsh". The sons and daughters of Wales were not so foolish as to confine themselves to the narrow limits of the Principality. (Hear, hear).

Sir Samuel's Response To Archdeacon Griffiths

Samuel Griffith, rising to respond,was received with much enthusiasm. No doubt, he said, as soon as the cheers had subsided, had been allowed to enter his mind since the day of arrival at Cardiff as to the warmth of the welcome he was to receive in Wales. From that moment to the present nothing could surpass the kindness with which he had been treated,and a bond had been created between the country of his adoption and the country from which he had originated. After further remarks expressive of the same sentiments, he spoke of the many Welshmen who lived in Queensland, a great many of whose industries were akin to those of Wales, and then went on to allude to the subject of a closer connection between Britain and her Colonies, which had caused the representatives of the Colonies to be summoned to London. Some years ago, he continued, a considerable party of British politicians had favoured the notion that the distant dependencies of the Empire should cast themselves adrift. There were still some distinguished men who held to those views, but they formed a very small minority, an almost inappreciable minority. (Applause).

The future of the Empire depended, to a great extent, upon the manner in which the different members of it were brought into union and communion. At present they were not so well acquainted one with the other as they ought to be. This was the sentiment, too, in England, wherever the subject was intelligently approached, but unfortunately, ignorance largely prevailed, and only occasionally did opportunities arise for dispelling that ignorance. The time was not ripe for creating a formal bond of unity. Still the present relations, which left the Colonies much in the same position as foreign countries,admitted of great improvement.

Besides the great bond of sentiment, the material one of trade—there was an axiom that trade followed the flag—united the motherland and her dependencies, and this latter supplied a sufficient answer to those who would cast the Colonies adrift .

He held that the Colonists should be regarded quite as absolutely members of the Empire as the people who lived in the three kingdoms. A reference to the question of the preservation of racial distinctions led on to a statement that Australians boasted of their power of absorbing and fusing in one harmonious commonwealth the peoples of all countries. They, too, had the cry of "Australia for the Australians" but this had a restricted meaning, and had prejudicial application only to those who regarded the country merely as offering advantages for exploitation and the making of rapid fortunes intended to be spent elsewhere. There was ample accommodation for those who were willing to work,but in assisting to solve the great problem of relieving the congested cities of England there was the difficulty of transferring a class of people to a country where the conditions of living and labour were totally different.

Sir Samuel gave a review of the progressive legislation of Queensland, which had provided for manhood suffrage, a simple method of transferring land, universal education by the State, and a system of local option, and then, after reminding the meeting that he was the leader of the Queensland Liberal Party, with Radical tendencies, he proceeded by inference to treat of the Home Rule question. Anything, he said, that might tend to weaken the bonds which united the Empire would be injurious to the Colonies; anything that would change the centre of gravity in the central body would be a very serious thing. Nothing could be more dangerous for the interests of the Empire than a change of this nature. The Colonists, consisting almost entirely of settlers from the three parts of the (United) Kingdom, looked upon the latter as their old home, and were content to be ruled by the Imperial Government. Assuming anything happened which should change the constitution of the United Kingdom, they could not possibly look with equal satisfaction upon a Parliament made up of the representatives of only one or two of the three kingdoms. Such a thing as that would make an essential change in the whole constitution of the British Empire. (Loud applause).

A very great number of the Colonists of Australia would not care or like to acknowledge the Supremacy of such a Parliament, in which they had no representatives of their own. That was a consideration which ought to be borne in mind, because of necessity there should be some central governing body. That was essential to the unity of the Empire.

The time had not yet arrived for federal representation, because with it taxes would have to be levied and powers created for executing the determinations of the Federal Government. He repeated that while they should desire to maintain,and if possible to strengthen, the unity of the Empire, anything tending to weaken the bonds of unity was a matter of most vital and serious concern.

At the same time he would add that the Colonists were accustomed to enjoy the utmost freedom and self-government to a degree which he should like to see extended to the people of this country. Before resuming his seat, he again spoke hopefully of the improved relations between the Imperial Government and the Colonies, and in gratefully acknowledging the warmth of his welcome, declared that every Welshman in Queensland would consider that he was personally honoured by the compliments and the honours they had showered on him. (Loud applause).

Further toasts were honoured, then the proceedings concluded.

The distinguished Cardiff journalist, Owen Morgan, (Morien), wrote a lengthy commentary on aspects of this Cardiff Banquet.

The following is an extract:–

"The eloquent Dean Vaughan makes, however, a woeful mistake if he supposes the people of Wales ever cry "Wales for the Welsh". What they say is, let not the Welsh be entirely neglected in their own country. When they advance this plea it is their enemies who have been in the habit of interpreting the cry to mean "Wales for the Welsh". It has been a kind of "Stop thief" cry, raised by a pickpocket running away after being detected perpetrating a dirty deed.

I was much interested to witness, when that noble son of Cardigan, Archdeacon John Griffiths, gently answered Dean Vaughan, the amused expression on the face of the Lord Bishop of Llandaff. A Bishop has to maintain on all occasions gravity, but on this occasion the Welshman in Bishop Lewis' nature was almost too powerful for the Bishop when the stentorian voice of Cardigan was heard declaring that the great Dean was mistaken when he supposed the Welsh ever cry "Wales for the Welsh". His Lordship found it necessary to hide the smile of St. Dubricius behind the episcopal hand. By this dexterity one fancies his Lordship is accustomed to the task of standing between the English and Welsh gladiators of the Church Militant in Wales."

The Departure of Sir Samuel Griffith

On Saturday morning Sir Samuel Griffith, the Premier of Queensland, left South Wales for London after what must have been an enjoyable visit to his birthplace.

Shortly before his departure, he was presented with a farewell Address from the Cymmrodorion Society, the following gentlemen comprising the delegation:– Archdeacon Griffiths, The Rev. G. A. Jones, Messrs. D. Isaac Davies, David Watkin Jones, (Dafydd Morganwg), E. Thomas, (Cochfarf), T. W. Lewis, T. T. Jones, O. L. Roberts, D.Beynon, B. G. Evans, Degwel, D. B. Davies, Evan Owen, Major Jones.

The Address was illuminated and was surmounted by the Queensland coat of arms. In a scroll was contained the inscription in Welsh:– "Cas nis caro, r'wlad a'i maco", which may be freely translated by Sir Walter Scott's well-known lines

Lives there a man with soul so dead
Who never to himself has said
This is my own,my native land?

"Dafydd Morganwg" read the Address,which was inscribed in Welsh, and English translation accompanying it. The Address which was couched in terms of sincerest respect, spoke of the pleasure which all Welshmen felt at seeing a native of the Principality elevated to the highest position in the Legislature of one of the most flourishing and successful Colonies belonging to Great Britain.

Merthyr Tydfil had been the birth-place of several eminent men, but none had given them such noble political rank as Sir Samuel, whose honourable position gave a national dignity to Wales and the Welsh nation. The fact that he had christened his son by the name Llewelyn ap Griffith was a gratifying proof that he still retained a Welsh heart, that Welsh blood coursed through his veins, and that he felt no inclination to disown the relationship with his mother country. The Address concluded with the hope that Sir Samuel might long be spared to enjoy his present honourable position.

Sir Samuel Griffith, in reply, said that the presentation of such an Address gave him a peculiar pleasure,from the fact that it so thoroughly represented the Welsh-speaking community. He had many Welsh friends in Queensland, who would be very gratified to read its purport.

Referring to the subject matter of the Address,he said that the great work of Colonial legislation must be an endeavour to succeed in making the country attractive to emigrants. This task both he and his colleagues in the Government of Queensland felt to be a very responsible one,but the effort would not be lacking on their part. He would long remember his visit to South Wales, and he really felt he did not deserve all the kind things that had been said of him.

Biographical Account

The following biographical account and character sketch of Sir Samuel Griffith appeared in the Merthyr Express newspaper in 1887:–

"Some men are born great, some achieve greatness, and some have greatness thrust upon them", so sang the immortal bard of Avon, and his words have been handed down as a maxim containing a world of meaning.

Sir Samuel Walker Griffith, K.C.M.G., Prime Minister of Queensland, a Merthyr lad, was neither born great nor did he have greatness thrust upon him. By his own industry alone, by his own energy, by his own perseverance, by his own talent, has he gained that distinction which sits so well upon him, and does so much honour to the town that gave him birth.

The son of a Nonconformist minister, Samuel Walker Griffith was born at Merthyr Tydfil on June 21st. 1845. His father, the Rev. E. Griffith, who was once pastor of Market square Congregational Church, emigrated to Australia in 1854, and was inducted to the charge of the Congregational Church at Ipswich. He subsequently laboured at Maitland and Brisbane, securing by his earnestness and assiduity the respect and love of some of the largest congregations in Queensland.

The future Prime Minister received his early education in Sydney. He subsequently graduated to the High School of Maitland,and in 1860 went to Sydney and there entered the University. In 1863 Sir Samuel was articled to Mr. Macalister,the leading solicitor at the time in Brisbane, and while an articled clerk, carried off the Mort Travelling Fellowship. He afterwards made a trip to Europe, and at the completion of his articles joined the Queensland bar in October 1867, and as barrister won great distinction. In 1872 he first entered Parliament; in August 1874 he was appointed Attorney-General in the Macalister administration. In 1876 he became secretary of Public Instruction; in 1877, secretary for Public Works. In the General Election which followed,

Sir Samuel was returned at the head of the poll. As a leader of the Liberal minority, he, for nearly five years, was the head of the opposition party. In 1883 the M'Ilwraith administration resigned, and Sir Samuel Griffith was pointed to as the worthiest and fittest politician to form a ministry. This he did, undertaking himself the offices of Premier, Colonial Secretary and Secretary for Public Instruction. These positions he continues to hold.

The Australian magazine, ONCE A MONTH, had some time ago an interesting biographical article from which the following masterly delineation of Sir Samuel's characteristics is culled:–

"Mr.Griffith is not a Parliamentary orator in the sense in which Mr. John Bright, the Marquis of Salisbury, or Mr. Sexton is. He is a ready debater, incisive in his indiction, and logical rather than argumentative. On occasion, however, he has delivered speeches which for close reasoning, apt illustration, and sustained power, would rank high in any of the great Legislative Assemblies of the world. Standing in an easy, almost careless, attitude in front of his despatch box, placed not on the table, but on the bench whereon he sits, he addresses himself alternately to the Speaker and to the front Opposition bench, in quiet, even tones. His utterance is rapid but clear, and when goaded by taunts and jeers of political opponents, his hard though not harsh voice is capable of exceeding scornful modulation, emphasised by a contemptuous wave of the hand in which he holds his papers, the only gesture he indulges in. He is never caught napping or tripping. We have seen him leaning back on his bench apparently asleep, or sitting at the table writing letters, as if he were oblivious of the course of the debate. But not a point of the Opposition argument had been lost. He would jump to his feet and take up and powerfully reply to every statement which had been made against him or his policy. As a Parliamentary tactician he has no equal in the Queensland Legislature. His capacity in this respect was never more fully manifested than in his conduct of the Land Bill through the Assembly, in the face of a compact, well organised and persistent opposition; and in his conciliatory attitude in the Conference between the Council and Assembly, when there was a possibility that a too unyielding stand might destroy the whole work of the session and lose the measure on which he had evidently set his heart. His skill won for him the admiration, not alone of his followers, but of the Opposition; and we know of nothing finer in political warfare than Mr. Hume Black's ungrudging testimony, at the close of last session,to the consummate ability of the man whom he had so determinedly opposed at every hand for over six weary months.

"We are all proud of him; Queensland is proud of him; Australia ought to be proud of him", said Mr. Black. As a capable administrator, Mr. Griffith has few equals. His power of work is phenomenal. He has the knack of reading the driest of blue-books at a glance,and picking out the salient points. Nothing escapes him in administrative detail; his grasp of political principle enables him to generalise accurately and swiftly from the most minute and often times discordant particulars.

In personal appearance Mr. Griffith is a tall and fair man, with sharply cut and not unhandsome features. His expression is self-contained, approaching to hardness. His manner is cold and unsympathetic. He is as reticent as Lynd-hurst, as impassive as Disraeli. It is said,however, that when in the society of intimate friends his constrained demeanour disappears, and that he becomes genial and pleasing. He is nothing of a conversationalist, but has a grim sense of humour, though he never personally indulges in it.

Finally, it is alleged that he is of that temperament which readily takes men as they seem, but that, when once suspicion is roused, he has too little regard in his judgments to the inherent weaknesses of human nature. These faults, if faults they be, are but the specks which by contrast enhance the purity and brightness of the amber. Mr. Griffith is a strong and commanding personality, destined to attain to yet greater triumphs, and to sway in no in considerable degree the future of Australia."

Sir Samuel Griffith (1845-1920) subsequently held the following Offices:– Queensland Premier 1883-88 and 1890-93. Queensland Chief Justice 1893. Queensland Lieutenant Governor 1889-1903. Chief Justice of Australia 1903-1919.

Morlais Morgan,
a Dowlais Boy

by ANN LEWIS AND MARGARET LLOYD

At Bethel Chapel, Georgetown in 1864, the lovely young Jane with beautiful red hair, married Thomas Morgan. They settled at Pengarnddu and later moved to Top Dowlais.

1. Pengarnddu in its hey-day

They had nine children but due to the hardships of the time only six survived. Jane was blessed with an excellent contralto voice and sang as she worked as a haulier on the tips near her home.

2. "Jane the Haulier"

The shawl around her shoulders was called a turnover. Her children grew up surrounded by music and this story is about two of her boys and their families: Morgan Morgan, born 1879, and his brother Evan Morgan who was two years his senior. As young lads their joy was to compete in Eisteddfodau. They had to borrow money for the entrance fees to enable them to attend, and because they possessed such fine voices they almost always won the prize money, which was given to them in little purses. They enjoyed competing against their brothers sisters and friends to see who won the most purses. Both the boys worked at local levels.

3. "Coal level where the boys worked"

While they worked I am sure they would have dreamt of becoming professional singers. They were both invited to join the Philharmonic Society whose conductor was the famous Mr. Harry Evans. Each member was issued with a membership card.

4. "Card of the Philharmonic Society. Conductor Mr. Harry Evans (1876)"

This choir went on to win the National Eisteddfod in 1900. Morgan Morgan almost missed that Eisteddfod by arriving late to catch the boat that was taking them to Liverpool. He could see the boat moving out! You can just imagine how he must have felt, but so like a true Dowlais man, he took off his hat and started to sing. The Captain heard him, lowered a small boat to go back and pick him up, so saving the day.

Morgan married a local girl and they had five children. They moved to the Rhondda Valley in 1906. In 1907 as Principal Baritone of the Rhondda Male Voice Choir, he toured America with them and was acclaimed "The Prince of Baritones". Morgan and another singer Parry Jones were fortunate to survive the sinking of the Lusitania in 1915 when many lives were lost .

He was the winner of two silver championship cups, the Rhymney and Gwent Eisteddfod of 1903/4, the Merthyr Eisteddfod of 1903/4 and many other prizes too.

5. "Morgan Morgan"

He won a scholarship to the Royal College of Music, London. Money was in short supply so he had to hold a series of concerts throughout the valleys to raise the money to support himself and his family.

One concert was held at the Hippodrome, Tonypandy in April 1924, another at the Oddfellows' Hall, Dowlais on May 10th. Morgan Morgan then wished to be known as Morlais Morgan: So on 14th May 1924, off he went to London leaving his wife and children behind.

He trained under an Italian teacher who advised him to become a tenor owing to the wide range of his voice but Morlais Morgan would have none of this. He remained a baritone. At the age of 48 years he became a professional singer. Doing well, his wife and children joined him in London and he was happy to find them employment outside the collieries; a great achievement in those days, having worked practically all his life in the mines, he wanted more for his children.

For those of us who have seen the film "Proud Valley", our Morlais Morgan was one of the singers coming out of the colliery. He sang alongside the great Paul Robeson, also that lovely Welsh soprano Megan Thomas. He also sang in London's West End long running show "Chu-Chin-Chow". In the 1920's and 30's he appeared in the Royal Albert Hall and frequently broadcast for the B.B.C.. He also did a phenomenal amount of charity work over the years.

Most of his recordings (and he made many) were recorded in 1929 and 1930, both in Welsh and English. During the Second World War he travelled to France and the Middle East with E.N.S.A. to entertain the troops. Of the sixteen people who formed the choir, two had Dowlais connections: Morlais Morgan who was born here and Nancy Ellis, born at Glyn Neath who married Tommy Bateman from Station Terrace, Top Dowlais, an Aunt and Uncle to Jean Phelps from the Pant Post Office. Nancy Bateman won a blue ribbon in the National Eisteddfod and often competed against her mother who was also a fine singer. Unfortunately Nancy didn't make any recordings, it was one of her greatest regrets. She stated that the choir was lucky to come out of the war alive. During the Blitz, Morlais's Fulham home in London was bombed and he returned to Dowlais for a short while.

After the war, his brother Evan's son Morlaisydd and his daughter Betty recall visiting Morlais at his London home. Waiting on the doorstep, he saw them coming. This fine figure of a man dressed in a white suit with a big hat and silver top walking stick stepped out into the middle of the road and broke into song to greet them: What a way to bring London's traffic to a halt! A true artist would you say?

Even at the age of 79 years Morlais still possessed a fine rich voice (recording still available) but what a struggle it had been for him to become a professional singer and recording artist. One of the many songs he recorded was the "Floral Dance" which was fairly recently a "Top Twenty Hit" when Terry Wogan sang it.

Some of Morlais's family are still living in London. But what of Morlais's brother Evan? He chose to marry and remain in Penywern, Dowlais. They had six children who were all blessed with musical talents. The three that stand out to me are Haydn born 1899, Morfydd born 1903 and Morlaisydd born 1904.

6. "Photograph of Evan Morgan and Family"

Many of us remember Haydn Morgan as an Ambulance driver who lived with his wife Ann and daughters Eirfron and Mairwen at Gwladys Street, Pant.

Trained by Mr. W.J. Watkins he possessed a tenor voice of rare quality- had he been in the least bit ambitious he would, like his uncle have become famous.

As a young man he competed against Haydn Adams Morgan and sometimes won in Eisteddfodau all over South Wales. Later Haydn Adams

Morgan changed his name to Haydn Adams by dropping the Morgan in order to shorten it. He sang on the Welsh Home Service and the Western Region from 1929-1962/3. His son and daughter-in-law, Mr. and Mrs. Kenneth Adams Morgan still reside in Merthyr Tydfil. Haydn Morgan was a talented man. He enjoyed painting in oil and water colours and sketched in pencil and charcoal.

7. *"Painting of Penywern Lane by Haydn Morgan"*

It was in his nature to help others in crisis as the need arose. His devotion to the St. John's Ambulance Brigade was an expression of this. After his death his daughters found he had written a history of the Dowlais St. John's Ambulance Brigade which confirmed it as the Wales No. 1 Division, an honour always claimed by Cardiff. Haydn was totally overcome when he was honoured to become Superintendent of the Dowlais St. John's Ambulance Brigade on 25th June 1964.

Haydn's sister Morfydd, who worked for a time at the Co-operative shop, Pant, had a beautiful contralto voice. On Sunday 4th July 1926 at the age of 23 years, she became the first Merthyr woman to broadcast live from Merthyr on B.B.C. Radio in a concert from St. David's Church, Merthyr. The famous Mr. W. J. Watkins was organist, the soloists were Mr. W. T. Lewis and Cliff Jones.

Morfydd had been trained by Mr. W.J. Watkins who was organist of St. David's Church for many years. Few people could afford to own radio sets in 1926, so the friends and neighbours of Morfydd's family at Penywern sat on the street pavements to listen to her voice and concert being relayed on the only wireless set (radio) available in the area.

Morfydd married Brychan Evans from Pant Road, a keen football player who was capped five times for Wales during 1931-1932. Brychan's job took him to London where they became active members of the Wimbledon Welsh Society. Morfydd continued to use her musical talents by singing and acting in amateur productions. Both she and her husband died quite a few years ago. They had no children.

Morfydd's younger brother Morlaisydd was named after his famous uncle. I'm told that the name means "The Voice of the Sea". Although gifted with a superb baritone voice, he was un-trained due to the expense; his parents had already paid for Haydn's and Morfydd's training. He used his gifts as singer, musician, hymn writer and poet to benefit the local community.

A man that always composed something new to put into "The Book" for the Gamanfa Ganu. He once told his daughter that he couldn't sleep because of the music that filled his head. After the death of his wife Jenny, he lived with his only daughter Betty and her husband Bill.

Morlaisydd followed in the footsteps of his father Evan and Uncle Morlais when he was invited to join the Dowlais and Merthyr United Choir. This choir won 1st prize at the National Eisteddfod at Fishguard in 1936. Later the choir was invited to sing at the Queens Hall, London, on 31st October 1936. Because of the depression in the area in the 1930's, it proved difficult for the members of the choir to fund themselves for the trip to Fishguard, so besides saving pennies weekly, collections were made in the area in order to make the journey to Fishguard possible. Of the two hundred and twenty members taking part, eighty per cent were unemployed.

8. "The Dowlais and Merthyr United Choir 1936"

The expenses for the trip to the Queens Hall, London were met by the Lords Camrose and Kemsley who were in the audience. The Mayor, Alderman Lewis Jones, was deeply concerned about the plight of the unemployed in the area and through his efforts the journey to the Eisteddfod was made possible. On the night of the concert in London, he made an appeal on behalf of the "The Settlements" in the Merthyr area. These "Settlements" had been established five years earlier to help the unemployed. They supplied education, social, recreational and occupational facilities. During the summer season many were enabled to have a camping holiday either in the countryside or at the seaside.

There were also study circles, lectures, singing and dramatic groups, physical training and educational classes and a variety of useful crafts were arranged. The members of the choir laid a wreath at the cenotaph before attending the concert. The "Daily Herald" newspaper sums it all up with the headline: "Merthyr Choir Thrills London Audience".

Morlaisydd, like all members of the Morgan family was an active member of the Penywern Chapel. He had helped build the foundations of the gateway and also the Big Vestry during the 1921 strike.

9. "Penywern Chapel"

It is interesting to note that only two chapels in the area have the vestry in the front. The vestry cost £1,848 to build. Penywern Chapel has always been a hive of activity. They formed a choir in 1910/11 of just seventeen members. This number eventually reached one hundred and twenty. They were known as the "Penywern and Dowlais Male Voice Choir".

They won many competitions but their most treasured wins were the Eisteddfodau of 1927. The three chairs presented to their conductor Mr. Evan Thomas were donated to the chapel.

10 "Three Eisteddfod Chairs With Four Survivors of the Choir"

In the background to the chairs is the organ Morlaisydd played for over forty years.

A miner for many years he protected his hands by wearing gloves. Conductor of Penywern Chapel for many years he also helped teach the children at the Band of Hope each Tuesday. Several hymn tunes that he composed were published in the Gymanfa Ganu programmes. Many of the Gymanfa Ganus were held at Bethania Chapel, South Street, Dowlais on Easter Monday, when the local Welsh Congregational Chapels would meet under one roof to enjoy their musical festival of singing and worship.

The hymn tunes sung would have been chosen the year before and the members of each chapel would practice the tunes over the winter months in preparation. One of Morlaisydd's hymn tunes "Brychan" was included in the Cymanfa Ganu held at Moriah Chapel, Bedlinog on 22nd December 1974, the conductor was Mr. Alun Williams of the B.B.C. Cardiff.

Other activities held at Penywern Chapel were the Eisteddfodu each Christmas morning as well as "The Books" or "Operettas". One of the last ones held was "Zurka the Gipsy Maid", another was "Joseph" performed many years earlier at the Oddfellows' Hall, Dowlais to a packed audience.

11. The Last Book Performed—'Zurka The Gipsy Maid"

Morlaisydd lived and breathed music but a great deal of the music he wrote remained un-named and un-published which seems a shame.

One of his poems was included in Mr. Josh Powell's book "All Change" and is about the Dowlais he loved. Another poem he wrote expressed his innermost feelings when, like many other families, he was forced to move from his home, when the Council decided to improve the area. Heartbroken at having to leave, he penned these words:–

12. "Ivor Street, Dowlais"
"OLD IVOR STREET"

Who wants to forget Old Ivor Street
Where the homes were kept so tidy and neat

And people so friendly as we would meet
Surely, we cannot forget.

Built by the craftsmen of the famous John Guest
Always known everywhere to be the best
For they had learned their trade and passed the test
No we cannot forget.

Known at one time as the widest they say
With nine public houses and two chapels to pray
Could one have a better place to stay?
How can we forget?

Bandsmen, pianists and organists as well
(Keeping the Devil down in Hell)
For now and again his followers would swell—
Don't let us forget.

Looking back over fifty years and more
One recalls that house of ninety four
Where we thought we'd live for evermore.
How can we forget?

Goodbye then, old street for evermore
Oh, how we wish we could have an encore
But now for us it is a closed door.
We'll never forget.

After Morlaisydd's death in 1984, one of his pupils wrote of him, "I have an abiding memory of a sensitive talented man whose love and enthusiasm for music was infectious. I'm grateful for his patient encouraging attitude towards me in my formative years. I was lucky to have him as my teacher. He dropped a pebble into my pool of musical and poetic consciousness and I'm still enjoying the sound of the ripples. God gave speech to all but song to few."

Betty, his daughter, had a strong sense of family duty so forewent a professional career of her own. Whenever Uncle Morlais wrote to his nephew he always addressed the envelope thus:– Morlais Morgan, Baritone Vocalist, 94 Ivor Street, Dowlais. which reveals that music filled their lives.

Morlaisydd's grandson Brynach inherits many of the family's talents, so the golden stream of music that was started by Brynach's great-great grandmother Jane goes on. Thank you. MORLAIS MORGAN 1879-1963

Best Wishes to the Dowlais Male Voice Choir
By Morlaisydd Morgan 1974

Today is D-day and the stage is set
(Rhos and Llanelli are in the bet),
Pontardulais also are eager to win,
Three choirs at which no-one can grin.
The others too all as "Strong as can be",
And all anxious to bring down the fame of D.T.

But the boys of Dowlais,—all sturdy and strong
Will show Carmarthen to whom they belong,
Straight from a stock of the best Dowlais steel,
Tempered so hard that they'll make someone feel
That this was the atom they split years ago,
Myndiaew, boys bach, be there to the fore.

With Jack Richards in front, little Adams too,
Des and Les and the committee so true.
With eyes on those hands with magnet and magic
You'll prove to them all this choir's dynamic.

The Schubert's "Spirit' along on the stage
With the love of '"Mordaith" don't be in a rage.
And as one last wish,—Please don't forget
Those Magic Hands—then you'll win your bet.

The slide talk, with five recordings of Morlais Morgan's fine voice was first presented by Mrs. Ann Lewis and Mrs. Margaret Lloyd for the Merthyr Tydfil Historical Society on Monday 2nd October 1989 at the Merthyr Tydfil Technical College. It was Mr. John Davies of 'Adlanni Recordings". who first brought the name of Morlais Morgan to my notice by enquiring if I knew of anyone of that name. I hadn't, until a few years later when I met Betty and Bill Heffernan and the link was forged.

It is with grateful appreciation that I thank Betty and Bill Heffernan for their time and assistance in making this paper possible. Many thanks also for the loan of their precious photographs, poems, paper cuttings, letters and music so lovingly recorded. "Adlanni Recordings" is the label devoted to re-issuing Welsh recordings from the past, Glyddyn Mawr, Y Ffor, Pwllheli, Gwynedd LL53 6RR.

My thanks are also extended to:– Dr. Bryan Griffith, Southgate, London. Mr. and Mrs. John Davies, "Adlanni Recordings". Mr. John Owen. Dr. Fred Holley. Mr. Geraint James and Staff of Merthyr Library. Staff of Treorchy Library. The Rhondda Leader Newspaper. The Daily Herald Newspaper. Mrs. Jean Phelps, Post Office, Pant. Mr. Brynach Lloyd Heffernan, Lecturer at the Merthyr Tydfil Technical College.